PRAISE FOR **UNSTOPPABLE**

"One of Ralph Nader's finest efforts. A bold and lucid handbook for the future."
—Patti Smith

"Conservatives and liberals both look askance at the Leviathan state and realize that promises of 'doing good' often obscure the reality of 'doing well' at taxpayer expense. Those looking for opportunities for bi-partisan cooperation should look at the nexus of statism and cronyism. *Unstoppable* shows that opposing such corruption can bring activists of the right and left together to fight side by side."
—Grover Norquist

"Ralph Nader's timely book once again makes him prescient in his insights about American politics. His against-the-grain predictions of a Left-Right alliance is not just a hope, but it is grounded in emerging evidence."
—Cornel West

"Nader at his best-original, indignant, idealistic, and on the lookout for new political alliances and possibilities. A tonic for the cynicism that's poisoning the groundwater of our democracy."
—Robert B. Reich, Chancellor's Professor of Public Policy, University of California at Berkeley

"No American in recent decades has done more than Ralph Nader to construct a workable alliance between the principled Right and the sincere Left to salvage our country and our national prosperity, and *Unstoppable* outlines his vital mission."
—Ron Unz, former publisher of the *American Conservative*

"Even-handed, erudite, practical, and necessary, *Unstoppable* is Ralph Nader's most broadly accessible book yet. Harnessing his lifelong crusade for the public interest over the corporatist agenda, Nader's convergence manifesto wisely calls for Left-Right alliances with similar goals to shun abstract labels and unite for the common good. Nader's treatise is optimistic and patriotic. He demonstrably shows that effective Left-Right alliances aren't pipe dreams, but historic realities in need of strategic cultivation, for the sake of our future."

—Nomi Prins, author of *All the Presidents' Bankers*

"I read Ralph Nader for the same reasons that I read Tom Paine. He knows what he thinks, says what he means, and his courage is a lesson for us all."

—Lewis Lapham

"Thomas Jefferson fretted that, with the passing of the founding generation, the truer patriotism that he knew as the 'Spirit of '76' would be lost. He need not have worried. Ralph Nader has re-captured the founding faith with an inspired call for a Left-Right coalition of conscience on behalf of democracy, liberty, fairness and peace."

—John Nichols, Washington correspondent for
    the *Nation* and coauthor of *Dollarocracy*

UNSTOPPABLE

THE EMERGING LEFT-RIGHT
ALLIANCE TO DISMANTLE THE
CORPORATE STATE

UNSTOPPABLE

RALPH
NADER

NATION
BOOKS
New York

Published by Nation Books,
A Member of the Perseus Books Group
116 East 16th Street, 8th Floor
New York, NY 10003

Nation Books is a co-publishing venture of the
Nation Institute and the Perseus Books Group.

Books published by Nation Books are available at special discounts for
bulk purchases in the United States by corporations, institutions,
and other organizations. For more information, please contact the
Special Markets Department at the Perseus Books Group, 2300 Chestnut Street,
Suite 200, Philadelphia, PA 19103, or call (800) 810-4145, ext. 5000,
or e-mail special.markets@perseusbooks.com.

Designed by Trish Wilkinson
Set in 11.75 point Goudy Old Style

Library of Congress Cataloging-in-Publication Data

Nader, Ralph.
    Unstoppable : the emerging left-right alliance to dismantle the corporate
state / Ralph Nader.
        pages   cm
    Includes bibliographical references and index.
    ISBN 978-1-56858-454-6 (hardback)—ISBN 978-1-56858-455-3 (e-book)
1. Business and politics—United States. 2. Corporations—Political
activity—United States. 3. Right and left (Political science)—United States.
4. Democracy—United States. I. Title.
JK467.N34 2014
322'.30973—dc23   2014001991

10 9 8 7 6 5 4

*To the memory and writings of
Jonathan Rowe—insightful skeptic, optimist,
believer in the potential of Left-Right coalitions,
and a practitioner of what he preached*

*and to John Richard,
networker and extraordinary advisor
to civic reformers.*

Contents

Introduction

When thinking about the genesis of this book, I remember the days working in my family's restaurant. The premises were spacious: a long lunch counter and many booths filled with townspeople and jurors from the local county courthouse, summer residents at the local lakes and camps, salespeople and travelers driving along busy Route 44 in Connecticut. In those non–fast food days, family restaurants were conveners of talkers, not just eaters. There was much ado about local and larger politics, and lots of free associative talk about the Yankees–Red Sox rivalry or what was going on in the many factories lining the town's streets.

Working the counter and the booths was a great education. It was conversation central, with humor, ribbing candor, and the famous Winsted raspiness. People didn't hide their party affiliations, mostly Democrat and Republican, but they didn't pigeonhole themselves when they gave their opinions or rendered their judgments. They weren't all friends by any means, but they weren't enemies either, all speaking as companionable individuals in a small town where everyone knew each other's ethnicity, religious denomination, and business. I listened more than I talked; therefore I learned.

As a college student, I was a serious, inveterate hitchhiker, eventually using my thumb to cover thousands of free miles in many states to reach my destinations. Once I was in the front seat of the truck or car, it would have been discourteous to promptly fall asleep, no matter how tired I was. Besides, I found talking with the drivers was a way to learn. They each had their expertise, working experience, and homespun life philosophy.

Years later, in 1992, stereotyped politically as an ultraliberal, I ran a brief none-of-the-above presidential campaign in the New Hampshire primary. I had no ads and little money to spend on the four or five trips I made to the Granite state, but of the 342,131 total votes given in a crowded field, I received 6,312, or 1.85 percent. Here's the funny thing: there were *slightly more Republican* than Democratic votes in my total.[1] People were surprised and kept talking about this unexpected dual appeal. I wasn't surprised. I spoke specifically, naming names, and asking for improved health, safety, and freedom of information laws, to be provided by accountable government and corporations in a society where freedom and justice discipline each other, so we can escape license and tyranny. My positions were largely for the benefit of everyone, regardless of creed, ideology, color, race, or gender.

It is with this experience in mind, the fact that my campaign appealed strongly to people in *both* parties, that I wrote this book to explore the topic of convergence, which I take to be voluntary alliances for the common good by positive-spirited persons of the Right and of the Left. A major area of potential for building alliances comes from the deep aversion many people have to the wars of empire and corporate control over their lives, particularly the ever-tightening influence of Big Business on the mainstream media, elections, and our local, state, and federal governments. These power grabs are then turned against the people themselves in harmful and lawless manners. If you are looking for more explicit labels for who would be attracted to these alliances, I see them as *a coming together* on various specific objectives of people who call themselves conservatives, libertarians, liberals, progressives, Republicans, Democrats, Independents, Third Partiers, capitalists, socialists, or anarchists, or use any other labels free-thinking Americans choose for themselves.

Aren't such alliances doomed? The enduring but surpassable obstacles to such convergences will elicit rejections from people who think such alliances are foredoomed to failure. Such naysayers have not yet experienced the exuberance of seeing through the divide-and-rule tactics that tell us we are a sharply divided "red state–blue state nation." This book is addressed first to those people who are *not* knee-jerk rejectionists. It's meant for those who want to explore another beckoning pathway—one that can rescue our country from being driven further into the ground and turn it into a nation where many more of its inhabitants can fulfill their potential.

A danger that skeptics—but not only skeptics—promulgate is complacency, the idea that political divisions are set in stone, so rightists and leftists, for example, could never join hands no matter how bad things get. But maybe these people don't realize how bad things have already gotten in our country. After all, most people want safe food and drugs. They want to breathe clean air and drink clean water. They want their work to be rewarded with adequate returns for the necessities of life. This is true, for example, among Walmart workers, whether they label themselves as "liberal" or "conservative." They want clean elections and competitive candidates, who provide perceived differences and choices in their platforms. They want their taxes to be reasonable and used well for the common good in an efficient manner. They want some voice in decisions that affect them. They want peace, justice, and public safety.

Yet they don't believe they can do much to get these desirable things. Too many do *not* believe they can fight city hall, Washington, or Wall Street. Large majorities tell pollsters, including 74 percent of those polled in a 2000 survey conducted by *Businessweek*, that Big Business has too much control over their lives and that the Big Boys will always get their way in Washington.[2]

Therefore, as if the culture has taught them helplessness, they have ceased to believe in themselves. Or at least they act that way: they don't spend any time and energy with others to acquire some knowledge and skills with which to restore the sovereignty and rights of the people. The instructive American history of triumphs over abusive power, usually against the odds, is lost to them.

These are generalizations about people's attitudes, but they are fairly accurate about tens of millions of honest, humane, hard-working, self-described powerless Americans. I say "self-described" because this is how people have been taught to depict themselves. Years spent in our educational system, our culture, and our political structures nurture a sense of powerlessness from a young age. We neither learn civic skills nor experience civic practices in our schoolwork—classroom to community—nor do we think of ourselves after our school years as possessing any "freedom to participate in power," to paraphrase Marcus Cicero. Yet, as I shall strive to demonstrate, there is a consistent, profound consensus among the American people as to the many directions our society must pursue. To be sure, there are consistent and profound differences as well, but the former far outweigh the latter and should not be subordinated to them. We can move areas of consensus into realities once we deliberate at the concrete levels of daily life and experience. That is where the widespread understanding and belief in fair play comes into formidable focus.

At this point, readers may say that while people do have wide agreement on many ends, they often disagree vigorously on the *means* to those ends. They think this is what keeps people from getting together. After all, this disagreement spills into our elections and our councils of government, such as Congress and state legislatures. How you reach agreed-on ends is the devil in the details.

Well, let's get underway and see.

1

Convergence:
The Sporadic Coming Together of
Right and Left Against Corporatists

A Signal Convergence

"Strange Bedfellows," was the way the *National Journal* in 1982 described the coalition of environmental and conservative groups opposed to the Clinch River Breeder Reactor in Tennessee.[1] The Breeder Reactor Project seemed unstoppable from the time it was first authorized by Congress in 1970. It soaked up money as if there were no tomorrow. A total of $1.3 billion was spent before a tree was cleared at the ninety-two-acre site.[2] No matter, the project had powerful backers from the Nixon and Reagan White Houses to the enthusiasts on Capitol Hill. They were buttressed by legions of lobbyists from the nuclear industry and its construction and engineering allies spread over three states, all intent on partaking of this taxpayer honeypot.

Once underway, the Breeder Reactor became a classic juggernaut of the corporate state, protected by the secrecy of the Atomic Energy Commission and its officious patron, the Joint Congressional Committee on Atomic Energy. Designed to breed its own

1

electricity, the project was treated like a military endeavor. It was protected from open debate and any disclosure or oversight, lest it give credence to the critics who called it a "technological turkey" that bred runaway economic costs instead of electricity. These critics' doubts were enough to persuade President Jimmy Carter— who was a nuclear engineer—to cancel the Breeder because of the risk of nuclear weapons proliferation. The Breeder lobby, however, continued to push to restart the project through Congress while Ronald Reagan was president.

But in the early eighties, Arkansas Democratic senator Dale Bumpers had the political nerve to encourage a liberal/conservative coalition. Until then, environmentalists were active, but conservatives had not focused on the issue intensely, since it was somewhat distant from their usual concerns. Once they did focus, they formed a group with liberals, which named itself the Taxpayers Coalition Against Clinch River. That umbrella organization included the Friends of the Earth, the National Taxpayers Union, our Public Citizen's Congress Watch, the Council for a Competitive Economy, the International Association of Machinists and Aerospace Workers, the National Audubon Society, the Union of Concerned Scientists, and the Natural Resources Defense Council.[3]

Washington hands saw this as an improbable combination of Left and Right. Members of Congress—who might have been reluctant to support the campaign—realized this combo gave them cover from their ideological and political opponents back home, since they couldn't be targeted as identifying with either a liberal or a conservative side of the issue. Meanwhile, estimates of the project's total costs were going through the roof. Congress's own General Accounting Office reported them as $8.8 billion. A House subcommittee predicted a cost range from $5.3 billion to $9 billion. Both figures were a few light years from the official $400 million estimate in 1970, even allowing for inflation.[4]

The anti-Breeder coalition was uniquely operational. We met regularly; this was not a mere petition drive or open letter to

Congress with no follow-up. The conservative/libertarian members reached their fiscally conservative friends in Congress with arguments about runaway costs, while the environmental/consumer groups were arguing that Clinch River would create a "plutonium economy," which would generate large quantities of that lethal product in forms that could be diverted for crude nuclear weapons.

On October 26, 1983, this coalition won a stunning victory. The Senate voted 56–40 against any further funding for the Clinch River Breeder Reactor project, thus beating a furious lobbying effort from a corporate–government combination on the other side.[5] The civic coalition against the Breeder Reactor triumphed over the corporate state. On the losers' side, no one was more taken aback than the project's leading booster, the powerful, well-connected Republican senator from Tennessee, Howard Baker. On the winners' side, archlibertarian Fred Smith, one of the coalition leaders, told me that the decisive impact came from the linkage of economic and security arguments, together with the energetic idealisms of the two camps.

Three years later, another Left-Right coalition broke through the immense lobby of government contractors to enact a revised False Claims Act with the False Claims Amendment Act of 1986. In the words of its key sponsors, Republican senator Chuck Grassley of Iowa and Democratic congressman Howard Berman of California, the 1986 law "provides a means and an incentive for reporting fraud against the public treasury. For thousands of individual whistle-blowers, it offers the only alternative to fearful silence or the near certainty of terrible consequence. It protects and rewards those with the courage to cast their light in dark places. It levels the playing field in the contest between corporate greed and personal conscience."[6]

The act was first proposed by public interest lawyer John Phillips, and groups interested in protecting taxpayer dollars and assets came from both conservative and liberal camps. Phillips made the rounds on Capitol Hill and found support from Republicans and

Democrats whose votes passed the legislation in the House and in the Senate. Conscientious whistle-blowers began to come forward to expose tens of billions of dollars in corporate fraud on government agencies from the Pentagon to the Department of Health and Human Services. These silent-no-more patriots were compensated with a share of the recoveries secured by the Justice Department, which partnered with them. By 2012 more than $40 billion had been recovered by the act, of which over $21 billion was the result of the whistle-blower protections and incentives that were enacted.[7]

As Grassley and Berman declared, by making greed pay the price and integrity receive the rewards, deterrence was given a lift. They noted studies that estimated that the fraud deterred "runs into the many hundreds of billions of dollars."

These clear-cut victories led some of us to wonder what other working coalitions could be forged between what the media chose to call "unlikely allies." There was no lack of opportunities in the following years. Outspoken verbal support from both sides for drug decriminalization, fighting corporate welfare, reducing military spending, stopping further media concentration, opposing taxpayer-funded stadiums and arenas, and challenging excessively invasive scanning by airport x-ray machines were just a few of such common stands taken by prominent leaders and organizations. Taking on a bizarre taboo, Congressman Ron Paul, with a dozen Democrats and Republicans, sponsored a bill to legalize the growing of industrial hemp, a long fiber used to produce food, paper, clothing, car parts, and fuel. Hemp is stigmatized because it is unfairly associated with marijuana. What makes the whole issue bizarre is that it has been legal for years to import industrial hemp from countries like Canada, China, Romania, and France, yet we can't grow it here.

Many major changes can be accomplished in areas where self-described liberals, conservatives, libertarians, and progressives all agree on the goal, not because they are pushed to these stands by pressure groups, but because they feel it is the right thing to do. But beyond words, it requires what Republican Bruce Fein calls "advocacy without an agenda."[8]

But there are also major obstacles to such convergences. Notwithstanding common ground for many in the Left-Right spectrum over such matters as sovereignty-shredding global trade agreements, Wall Street bailouts, the overweening expansion of Federal Reserve power, and the serious intrusions of the USA PATRIOT Act against freedom and privacy, barriers to the transition from thought to action come from numerous directions and in many forms.

The Hijacking of the Conservative Label and the DNA of Corporatism

Write an article, as I have, in a widely circulated publication about such an alliance of Right and Left, and back comes a blizzard of buzzwords—an oft-repeated semantic wave whose ultimate purpose is to stop further discourse. You've heard them. Billions of dollars of propaganda over the past century have succeeded in making the two major political camps engage in chronic, if not knee-jerk, jousts against one another. Here are some of the conclusory and provocative charges designed to end deliberate, evidential thinking: "that's socialism," "anti-capitalism," "free market," "big government," "overregulation," "deregulation," "confiscatory taxes," "tort reform," "welfare," "against free enterprise," "stifles competition," "freedom of contracts," "tax and spend," "borrow and spend," "deficit spending," "job-killing legislation," "defense—whatever it takes."

Presently, the most effective of all buzzwords is the label "conservative," cleverly used by corporate power brokers to provide semantic cover for their radical strategic plan for the union of Big Business and many government institutions. Their actions have nothing to do with actual conservatism, but no matter. The word is more powerful than any deeds to the contrary. Take President Ronald Reagan's statement that he had a "conservative" agenda, namely, "a strong defense, lower taxes and less government." That he was not consistent—under his presidency there were much larger deficits, taxes reduced were later raised, and government grew—did not affect his image. He knew the hypnotic power of a slogan endlessly repeated.

Corporate lobbies, knowing a good thing when they see it, seize the label "conservative" to shield many very *unconservative* demands and policies. They have misleadingly exploited revered economic philosophers, such as Adam Smith, whom authentic conservatives draw on for justification, authority, and identity. But no matter how often these corporate commercialists call themselves conservatives, it is hard to mistake them for old-line conservatives since the two minds (corporate versus old-line) hail from very different moral, historical, and intellectual antecedents. Whereas true conservatives look back to Smith, Edmund Burke, and other major theorists as their forebears, corporatists' antecedents hail from the worshippers of Mammon and those who held and abused their wealth in the days of merchant power. True conservatives should disdain such precursors. Meanwhile corporatists ride on conservative coattails and claim as their own the old-line conservative thinkers.

Corporatism or "corporate statism," as Grover Norquist calls it, is first and foremost a doctrine of corporate supremacy. Whatever advances that system of power and status over the constitutionally affirmed sovereignty of the people comprises the widening, all-encompassing corporatist agenda. As befits the ever-concentrating command of ever more mobile capital, labor, and technology—as well as its own media—the corporations' dynamic of expanding control with ever more immunity knows no self-imposed limitations. Large corporations usually push, with whatever political, technological, economic, marketing, and cultural tools are required, the frontiers of domination in all directions. Wielding the tools to advance their agenda is an army of diverse experts and operators bound together by common economic interests within the authoritarian hierarchy of the modern global corporation. However you might describe them, it is hard to deny that their DNA commands them to control, undermine, or eliminate any force, tradition, or institution that impedes their expansion of sales, profits, and executive compensation. That is what their extensive strategic planning is all about. What they want is maximum predictability and the most feasible control of outcomes, with government being the preferred servicing or enforcement tool.

That is what is meant by corporate statism. And as it gets stronger, it delivers a weaker economy for a majority of Americans, a weaker democratic society, and record riches for the few.

Franklin Delano Roosevelt, though hailing from the patrician class, put his finger on the dangers of corporatism. He wasn't charitable in his message to Congress in 1938, successfully calling for the creation of a Temporary National Economic Commission (TNEC) to examine the concentration of corporate power. He averred that "the growth of private power to a point where it becomes stronger than [the] democratic state . . . in its essence is fascism."[9] Though World War II's Axis powers gave the word a more lethal meaning, Roosevelt was equating fascism with the corporate state, uniting corporate influence with, over, and inside the government at state and national levels.

In recent years, as trade, investment, and other relations between nations have tightened, the corporate state has heightened its international "governing" power through such transnational systems of autocratic decision making as the International Monetary Fund (IMF), North American Free Trade Agreement (NAFTA), the World Trade Organization (WTO), and various regional agreements. Corporate managed trade, with its many pages of self-serving rules, is not "free trade."

Neither of the Left Nor of the Right

Given the increasing influence of corporations, it hasn't taken corporate political strategists or their public relations firms long to see how powerful, if not decisive, alliances between the Left and Right can be in influencing Congress or other public bodies of decision-making. So one part of the corporate agenda is to get both sides fighting each other, so they are distracted from collaborating on shared goals, which would otherwise cause serious discomfort for corporatists. Corporations themselves, meanwhile, have no faith in these labels. We saw that seizure of the conservative label by corporate interests allows them to appropriate conservative philosophy and provides resources for its notable thinkers to degrade the image of the liberal label.

On the other hand, untroubled by ideological niceties, these expedient corporations do not hesitate to exploit and profit from programs uniformly identified with liberal politics, such as the war on poverty, Medicare, Medicaid, food stamps, and foreign aid. All these programs have proved to be extremely lucrative for corporations that contract with government agencies. Peter Schweizer of the conservative Government Accountability Institute has charged that the country's biggest corporations, including J. P. Morgan, are profiting from the explosive growth of these programs designed for the poor. "Welfare in America is supposed to be a safety net for those in need, but instead, it's become an insider's game of power and profit," Schweizer said, referring especially to the food stamp program's contractors like J. P. Morgan.[10]

Key to understanding corporate behavior is the recognition that, while its propagandists trumpet the irreconcilable differences between Right and Left, corporations are remarkably flexible in relation to these divisions. What is behind this plasticity is a laser-like focus on expansion, profits, and bonuses. Corporate behavior transcends the normal meanings of opportunism. Corporate action is easy because there is rarely any steadfast, internal, interfering moral compass in the way.

Heavily funding and pressing the two major parties into a duopoly of concessions to corporate demands, the leaders of Big Business, after an election change, have only to readjust their Washington Rolodexes for high-level contacts, if the new appointees to cabinet and subcabinet levels are not already their business buddies. Whether Democrats or Republicans are in control, corporations still receive the same wasteful or expanding assorted privileges and immunities, inflated contracts, and other perks of crony capitalism and weak law enforcement—though in an unerringly rising arc of money and benefits. This is some of what President Eisenhower was alluding to in his 1961 farewell address when the retired five-star general gravely warned the American people of the "military-industrial complex" and its threat to our liberties and well-being.

Even while the harmony between the business lobbies and the two major parties may occasionally be disrupted by either intercorporate conflicts or principled opposition from authentic conservatives and liberals/progressives, the well-budgeted corporate think tanks will continue to provide a torrent of selective ideological cover for the broader corporate agenda, with tactics like promoting rigid opposition to taxes and regulations. To the uninformed, these groups are proven masters of plausibility, offering covers for corporations' not-so-hidden agendas.

The counterweight put forth in this book relies on the supremacy of civic values to which commercial pursuits must adjust (what Adam Smith may have meant by his phrase "moral sentiments") and with which they can properly thrive.

Escaping the Labels

Moreover, there are more and more examples of Left-Right alliances coming forward every year. They rarely break through to achieve their objectives. But they are escaping the "pitiless abstractness" of their adopted theories and working in the world of reality in a way that both reflects and disciplines more concretely their general philosophies.

The evocative phrase "pitiless abstractness" comes from an experience that conservative columnist George F. Will had in the late 1970s.[11] While sitting at home in his Washington, DC, study, where he was writing his syndicated column, he heard a loud crash. Running out the door, he saw a woman lying on the street who had just lost her life in a vehicle collision. Returning later to his desk, he wrote that he had had enough of "pitiless abstractness" and, contrary to the Reagan position, declared his support for mandatory installation of air bags by auto manufacturers.

What Will did was to descend the abstraction ladder of general antiregulatory dogmas to the facts on the ground. He derived a life-saving principle—mandating long-tested safety technology—from the grisly remains on the street. Mr. Will had seen "the other."

Let's look at some other examples where Left-Right convergence occurred, often prompted by real-world experiences. In 2008, demands from both the Left and the Right on and inside Congress led that body to ban genetic discrimination by health insurers. This went against the position of the influential insurance industry and its allies. It would not have happened without this alliance testing its different principles in facing the injustice of any person, adult or child, being denied insurance based on a corporate classification of their birth genes.

Note the power of addressing concrete situations. Fred Stokes, a career army and Vietnam War veteran and a self-styled Southern conservative, was president of the Organization for Competitive Markets (OCM). OCM is a small, feisty, farmer-protection association that challenges the predatory behavior of large agribusiness suppliers (Monsanto seeds, fertilizers, etc.) and buyers (the giant grain and beef packing plants) that are squeezing small farmers and ranchers off the land or turning them into a modern form of contract peons. I helped start OCM and worked with others who call themselves liberal or progressive and who joined together with the farmers and ranchers. What is the common ground? A call for fair competition and enforcement of the 1921 Packers and Stockyards Act. Those in the group insist on the freedom to sell to and to buy from competitive, not concentrated or monopolistic, buyers and suppliers. OCM members sit largely to the Right of the political divide on social issues and military and foreign policy. But when it comes to their focus on active OCM issues, liberals and progressives collaborate with them because they're right on!

I found what might seem an even more surprising resonance in 1998, when I received an invitation to address a United Methodist Church convention in Washington, DC, about the conflict between corporate and conservative values. One of the frictions I described at length was the deliberate commercialism of childhood. There was the well-planned marketing strategy to sell unhealthy junk food and drink and violent, sadistic products and programming directly to young children, bypassing and undermining parental authority, day after day, everywhere. I called these relentless, harmfully addicting companies "electronic child molesters."[12] It did not take any time for the parents in the room to resonate with my description of how corporate advertisements are consciously designed to induce parental guilt and provoke constant requests by children to get their parents to buy the touted product. Madison Avenue advertising firms coined the bold phrase "high nag factor" to praise and reward creators of ads that produce a high rate of pestering from children. I received a vigorous ovation from an audience whose views on many other subjects, from government regulation to the choice of candidates seeking office, undoubtedly ran counter to mine. Those differences, however, did not detract from the common desire we felt to protect our children from avaricious motivations traceable all the way back to Mammon.

Indeed, another case where a marked conservative agenda inter-
sects with very liberal ideas comes in my next example. Few people
recognized this intersection because stereotypes lead to abrupt pre-
judgments and dismissals of people who are seen as being on the
opposite ends of the political spectrum. It is like not being able to
see the trees because the forest is distantly seen as a monoculture
when, given its microdiversity, it definitely is not. The example
that comes to mind is the 2002 Texas State Republican Platform. If
any political statement invites stereotyping, it would be that platform. Think: Republicans, Texans, George W. Bush, Dick Cheney.
In many of its planks, these self-described conservatives do not dis-
appoint. The platform calls for an end to the personal income tax,
inheritance tax, corporate income tax, payroll tax, and minimum
wage. It also calls for eliminating the Department of Health and
Human Services, Commerce, Labor, the Department of Education,
the Environmental Protection Agency, the Internal Revenue Service, the Bureau of Alcohol, Tobacco and Firearms, and, for good
measure, the "position of Surgeon General."

Remember, this is the state Republican Party that launched
George W. Bush's political career. Yet he was their president in
2002 when this platform demanded, along with its conservative
planks, that Washington repeal NAFTA and GATT and get out
of the World Trade Organization. It is adamant against any gathering, accumulation, and dissemination of personal data and information on law-abiding citizens by business and governments.
It wants "all citizens" to be free from government surveillance of
their electronic communications.

In a slam against then-president George W. Bush and Attorney
General John Ashcroft and the PATRIOT Act they pressed into
law, the Texas Republican Party believes that the "current greatest threat to our individual liberties is overreaching government
controls established under the guise of preventing terrorism." Then
taking aim at a core bastion of corporatism, the platform declared:

"The Party does not support governmental subsidies, tariffs, bailouts or other forms of corporate welfare [including sports stadiums] that are used to protect or preserve businesses or industries that have failed to remain relevant, competitive and efficient over time."[13] Recall that President Bush made his $14 million fortune by having Texas taxpayers pay for the Texas Rangers' new baseball stadium. Of course, this was minor play compared to the direct corporate welfare bailout he arranged for the Wall Street banksters in 2008.

There is an obvious explanation for the president's own state party platform containing so many planks directly opposed to what the White House was saying and doing. This document was the product of the motivated, workhorse libertarian-conservative wing of the Republican Party; it has similar comparisons with Republican state platforms in other Southern states.

It turns out the Republican Party has a double life: the main party dominated by corporatists and the adjunct party relying on conservatives and libertarians to produce the margin of votes for victory in elections. The corporatist Republicans let the libertarians and conservatives have the paper platforms and the core ideological issues, pat them on the back at party convention time, and then move into office, where they are quick to throw out a welcome mat for Big Business lobbyists with their slush funds, who are anything but libertarian or conservative in their demands.

Where Do Action-Inducing Ideas Come From, and What Are Their Effects?

The people who wrote this Texas platform view themselves as political inheritors of the ideas of the major conservative and libertarian thinkers and writers, relying on selected abstractions from these scholars to shape their understanding of politics. Yet most people who call themselves libertarian or conservative, like most self-styled liberals, are not politically active. (Later some emerged as the early

Tea Party activists.) Half of either camp does not even vote. But when it comes to elections, those who do go to the polls reliably vote for those candidates whose rhetoric is closest to their vernacular.

A common observation about how people come to self-select their political identities is that they mostly flow from regular daily experience, family upbringing, and the likes and dislikes they develop in life. They rarely come because they read Lincoln Steffens or Ayn Rand or listened to Rush Limbaugh or Jim Hightower. These personages largely serve to reinforce experiential and hereditary dispositions and prejudices. Reinforcement can either enrich and broaden one's beliefs or render them even more absolute and distanced from reality on the ground. In a bipolar political climate manipulated by the power structure, guess which of the foregoing effects is dominant when people tune out the other side?

It is instructive to note that when conservatism was at its lowest ebb as a movement in the early 1950s, William F. Buckley started the comeback by, in 1955, launching the *National Review* with the belief that ideas matter. Its pages were filled with conservative philosophy wrapped around calls for a stronger military defense to counter godless communism, the elevation of private enterprise over public investment, and the pushing back of the "heavy hand of government" from populist directions. The *National Review* was mostly routine corporatist fare in "conservative" garb.

Like Buckley, all movements of any import look for intellectual authorities, whether they are Ludwig von Mises or John Maynard Keynes, Adam Smith or Karl Marx. That's where they get their connected "Big Picture," with sweeping explanations and justification for the way the world works or should work. Call it "philosophy," "theory," "doctrine," or "dogma," but do not underestimate its value in solidifying adherents around a common perspective and quest. Such philosophies prove especially effective when they are systems of belief that are categorical and abstract in their content, as opposed to more flexible systems of thought that leave options open for revision and factual persuasion. The former are often called "ideology," while the latter are often termed "rationalism" or, at their apex, "science."

Ideological belief systems most often prevail over rationalist thought systems. Political, social, and religious movements attest to this point. But, as is widely known, the ascendance comes with a price exacted from the reality that does not fit the theory of its vested adherents. Theory has its place in helping to organize thought and feelings, motivate future trends, create values of right and wrong, and offer predictions of the future. But taken as dogmatic marching orders, which are not subject to regular discipline or exposed to refutations, theory becomes a barrier to free thought, flexible strategy, and tactics for action. It becomes a conceptual prison.

To circle back to a previous thought, I noted many good people want to believe in a framework, a set of abiding and directing values that makes sense to them. But these secular frameworks and opinions can end up harming more than helping, as they become so autocratic they prevent loyalists from testing their applications in the vortex of political debate and alliances. The next step is knee-jerk prejudgment and ostracism of others who wear different political labels. No meetings over lunch. No reading of each other's polemics. Just speak the slogans to the convinced.

We see that people who adopt a rigidity of this kind are easy prey for eager commercialists, those mega-builders of concentrated economic power, with their political servants and open checkbooks, who falsely label themselves conservatives. I have not met a conservative who calls himself a corporatist, but I have met many a corporatist who masquerades as a conservative—the better to forge a false communion with authentic conservatives as a way to increase the giddy power of the corporate state.

In these pages we explore a different kind of communion by taking labels and doctrines down the abstraction ladder until they fall away and reveal the common core of people's humanity, which finds expression in factual realities, and the many senses of fairness and fair play that appear right where people are interacting every day—their workplaces, neighborhoods, marketplaces, public spaces, and the all-encompassing physical environment. This inquiry does not expect that people will shear off from their political beliefs and values and become factual ethicists. Humans cannot live by facts alone. But embracing facts informs beliefs and judgments and gives values the grounding for possibly greater meaning. As Aldous Huxley, author of *Brave New World*, declared, "*Facts do not cease to exist because they are ignored.*"[14]

People's Shared Values:
Envisioned But Seldom Put into Practice

Consider, for example, Walmart workers. They may label themselves liberal/progressive or libertarian/conservative, but there are some things they could agree on. About a million Walmart workers either make between $7.25 and $10.75 an hour or are required to work considerably less than forty hours per week at or above $10.75, so that they earn less than $10.75 times forty hours a week. The CEO, Mike Duke, works full-time and makes $11,000 an hour plus benefits.[15] Don't they want some job security and the benefits workers have in many other Western countries? Don't they also want a voice in decisions that affect them? But too many do not believe they can even join together to demand that Walmart give US workers the fairness and respect that Walmart *by law* must give its workers in Canada or Western Europe. They are not unlike the self-labeled liberals and conservatives (LibCons or LCs) who, for the time being, have ceased to believe in themselves as citizens who can make a difference.

Is the sense of futility of the average Walmart worker surprising? Since they were youngsters, our educational systems, atomized culture, and top-down oligarchic structures urged on them a sense of powerlessness. Whether as children or adults, these workers absorbed little sense of civic history, local or national; they weren't exposed to stories of those aggregated community activities in the past that have produced what is freer, fairer, and most democratic about our society. But those who have fought for democratic freedoms knew something that is being forgotten. Freedom should be described, they knew, as the Roman Marcus Cicero defined it: "Freedom," he wrote, "is participation in power."

Bearing in mind what Abraham Lincoln called the importance of "public sentiment," let us note that at the concrete levels of daily life, with its deprivations, fears, hopes, and joys, when people are faced with factual choices and possibilities, undisguised by the wrappings of "pitiless abstractness" and generalized theories, they expect fair play, the essence of the Golden Rule. At this level, shucking ossified theories about human behavior, open minds band together against the few, driven, monetized minds that are deciding for the many the determinants of their livelihood. Open minds stand against those ever hungry to take away our constitutional power and concentrate it against us, those plutocrats and oligarchs who perfect flexible tools of control that would have frightened but not surprised Thomas Jefferson and Abraham Lincoln, who grimly foresaw the dangers of the few gaining too much power.

As noted, people do have wide agreement on many ends, though they may disagree vigorously on the timing or pathways to those ends. From Walmart workers to nurses to schoolteachers, who doesn't want peace and prosperity, honest government and honest corporations, fair taxation, less waste, and more opportunity? They are right to want those things, but they are seeing them from the ground. The competing, self-styled intelligentsias who fill our media do not normally start there. Their minds contest on the plane of principles, philosophies, ideologies, or doctrines, while they ignore the details—most of the details, that is, except who pays the piper.

A Tale of Three Senators

I saw this last point, about the important detail of who has a vested economic interest in a given outcome, play out in a visit to Senator Strom Thurmond at his storied office one afternoon in 2002. Its walls were filled to the high ceilings with signed photographs of presidents and other notables, proclamations, certificates, and plaques commemorating a half century in the US Senate. If Strom Thurmond was known for anything, it was his championing of states' rights, which is the idea that the federal government should not interfere with a state's prerogatives. That's why I was sitting across from his desk that afternoon. The Senate was considering legislation that, if enacted, would federalize and therefore preempt the states' historic common law of torts in the area of medical malpractice (S. 1370). I argued the case on conservative and historical grounds, echoing his own career-long rhetoric on the subject and noting the opposition to this bill by his longtime colleague, recently retired Democratic senator Fritz Hollings. Senator Thurmond listened politely and replied that his concern about the bill was the danger of "frivolous" malpractice litigation in the states, to which I factually responded that this fear had little supportive data and was being handled by state judges when they see it. He didn't say outright that he was voting for federalization. However, he later voted on the Senate floor, on the losing side, to allow the Senate to consider preempting state malpractice laws. The medical industry had long ago gotten him on their side. That seemed the one detail that was important to him.

An instructive contrast rests with the change of mind that Senator Hank Brown adopted just before the crucial Senate vote to approve the World Trade Organization (WTO) in 1995, when Bill Clinton was its supportive president. The story starts with feedback I was getting after visiting numerous members of the House and Senate to persuade them to oppose the WTO. It became clear that neither the senators, nor the representatives, nor their as-signed staff on the matter demonstrated any assurance that they had read the five-hundred-fifty-page treaty, called a "trade agree-ment" by Mr. Clinton to avoid the two-thirds vote required by the Constitution for treaties.

The people on Capitol Hill had a year to read through what was the largest single surrender of local, state, and national sovereignty in US history. All treaties involve giving up some sovereignty, but this one was the grand slam and it had enforcement teeth. The WTO, conceived largely in secret between government officials and corporate lawyers, was sent to Congress on an autocratic fast-track procedure prohibiting amendments and severely limiting time for debate. Antidemocratic autocratic procedures predictably lead to autocratic outcomes. With the enforcement tribunals in Geneva, Switzerland—closed to the press and public—the WTO embraced far more than trade, as Global Trade Watch director Lori Wallach has pointed out, reaching into so-called nontariff trade barriers, like countries having higher consumer, environmental, and worker pro-tections than other signatory nations.[16] Having such protections got your country in trouble with WTO rules, which would have the force of federal, though not constitutional, law in the United States the moment our government signed on. Higher safety, health, and economic protection standards could be challenged by countries with lower or no such regulations as barriers keeping out their ex-ports of automobiles, food, chemicals, endangered species, fauna and flora, medicines, and more. Our courts, regulatory agencies, and legislatures are bypassed by these unelected Geneva tribunals from which there is only an internal, not an independent, appeal from the WTO decision. Punishment could be fines, trade retaliations, and demands for outright repeal of the offending superior national or state standards.

Senator Hank Brown called himself a free trader. As a conserva-tive Republican from Colorado, he had voted for NAFTA in 1993.

One day in 1994 he received, as did all other members of Congress, a challenge letter from me. I would give a $10,000 contribution to the lawmaker's favorite charity if they would sign an affidavit certifying they had read the entire text of the WTO treaty and then would be willing to answer questions about its contents in a public forum open to citizens and the media. Only Senator Brown replied, and while he did not want the donation made, he accepted the challenge. About two weeks later, in the Senate Foreign Relations Committee meeting, with the reporters and camera people ringing the room, he answered all twelve questions accurately. He then declared that, as a free trader, he was so appalled by the antidemocratic provisions within the WTO agreement that he was going to vote against it and urge everyone else to do so.

Why did he vote against it? Because Hank Brown went from the abstract slogan—free trader—and immersed himself in the realities of what the WTO was: a transnational, secret, autocratic system of control inimical to our democratic system of governing, which includes open courts. He went down the abstraction ladder and found that his fundamental conservative principles of prudent public governance were violated in powerful and varied ways. He saw that hundreds of pages of rules were in effect regulations without recourse, pressures on the United States for often having higher standards than many of the other 128 country signatories to the agreement. It is remarkable how doing one's homework can correct stereotypical thinking.

Take conservative Iowa Republican senator Chuck Grassley. I went to see him in 2007 to ask for his leadership, given his seniority on the Senate Finance Committee, in pushing faster for legislation he supported that would require the full text of all federal contracts (above a minimum amount) be placed online for all to read, report, scrutinize, or challenge. Before I got started, he asked, "What's going on with your Democrats?" He had just come from a committee meeting where "liberal" Democrats Chuck Schumer of New York and John Kerry of Massachusetts opposed his position requiring hedge funds to pay taxes on their commissions as ordinary income rather than the present, much lower 15 percent capital gains rate. He left little doubt that he believed Wall Street had gotten to them.

Corporatism, which so often targets conservatives, is increasingly targeting so-called liberals and creating the opposite type of convergence than the one this book is promoting. This sinister convergence between Democrats and Republicans beholden to the corporatist message often confounds outside citizen groups, who expect a greater difference between liberals and conservatives in this two-party duopoly.

All these overlaps can become confusing, which is why one quest in this book is to pull back the curtain of corporate camouflage and political duplicity. People need more awareness of how corporate pressures lead to the forked tongue of elected men and women. While this book notes and recommends a convergence on the common ground of increased democracy and people's power, it also records the mirror image at the top, where so-called conservative and liberal politicians forget their labels when they join together at the trough of corporate largesse on the way to fronting for the corporate agenda.

2

Conservatism's Authority Figures: Principles Versus Dogmas

If all the revered conservative philosophers agree on one principle, it is that conservatism is not a dogma, not a catechism, not a rigid belief system—as they accuse Marxism of being. They believe in liberty too much to even want a system of prescriptive rules. Rather, they see conservatives as attaching primacy to established institutions, traditions, and orderly ways that have met the test of time and temper while viewing with keen skepticism any untested, upsetting ways of thinking and doing.

Since established ways and institutions usually reflect the existing distribution of power, wealth, and property, conservatism has been associated with societies where the few dominate the many, ultimately through the use of the police force when all other silent and overt repressions fail. Plutocrats and oligarchs attach themselves to the label "conservative."

Nonetheless, conservatism has received a bad rap over the past century, and its philosophers have been misused, distorted, and sometimes willfully mischaracterized in order to propagandize the public mind and cover crass commercialism with a moralistic, philosophical camouflage.

Adam Smith, First Victim of Corporatist Mishandling

Has any moral philosopher and political economist been more manipulated by the power brokers than Adam Smith? In their war against regulation (critics would say against "law and order"), taxation, and government spending, combined with their defense of bigness, monopolies, and oligopolies, and their imbalanced use of the law to their advantage, corporatists have cited Adam Smith's "invisible hand" over and over again.

Writing in England about the time of the emerging American revolt, Smith produced two prodigious achievements, *The Wealth of Nations* (1776) and *The Theory of Moral Sentiments* (1759). They reflected an immensely nuanced mind able to conceive thoughts from the constants of human nature, nourished by social and individual morals and sympathy, and a deep understanding of the realities of the emerging industrialization and merchant trade of Britain with nearby nations. At the time, the use of large joint-stock companies—limited liability firms owned by shareholders—was breaking down the old order of agrarianism and craftsmanship. Smith's suspicion of government regulation proceeded significantly from his belief that such restraints favor the privileged interests that want to entrench their economic advantages through the force of law. (In the twentieth century, this belief was updated as "regulatory capture" by famed University of Chicago conservative economist and Nobel laureate George Stigler.) More prophetically, Smith foresaw what Robert Monks described as "four underlying dangers in the joint stock company, predecessor to the modern corporation. He observed that these entities tended to seek: unlimited life, unlimited size, unlimited power, and unlimited license."[1]

Smith, way back in the eighteenth century, worried about these managers "of other people's money" and the separation of ownership from management's controls.

The Wealth of Nations argued that high wages were both economically and morally beneficial, compared to the "bad effects of high profits." Smith wrote: "No society can be flourishing and happy, of which the far greater part of the members are poor and miserable. It is but equity, besides, that they who feed, clothe and lodge the whole body of the people should have such a share of the produce of their own labor as to be themselves tolerably well fed, clothed and lodged."[2] He tore into any business collusion, telling his readers to watch out whenever a group of businessmen get together. An early forecaster of the corporate state, Smith asserted: "Civil government, so far as it is instituted for the security of property, is in reality instituted for the defense of the rich against the poor, or of those who have some property against those who have none at all."[3]

Smith's "invisible hand" metaphor flowed from his approval of markets so decentralized or *de-monopolized* between sellers and buyers that the cumulative choices, however self-interested, would redound to the larger common good. His approved role of government, other than defense against external enemies, was to administer justice in disputes, invest in "certain public works and certain public institutions" (including "basic education at the parish level"), and regulate prices for essentials, such as foodstuffs, where they were in the grip of a monopoly. He would have been shocked to learn of his conversion into the patron saint of giant corporate capitalism and its professional apologists.

Ludwig von Mises, Second Only to Smith in the Conservative Pantheon

While at times very distorted, the ideas of major scholars and thinkers deemed conservative ring through the ages, from Edmund Burke (defend the cumulative wisdom), to David Ricardo (free trade), and on to Friedrich Hayek (road to *state* serfdom), and their later twentieth-century successors, notably Frank Meyer, Peter Viereck, Russell Kirk, and Murray Rothbard, among others. Though it is not quite as argument-clinching as is the scripture cited by devout Christians, in fervent conservative circles there is a similar citing of words from a hierarchy of revered thinkers, each with their schools of thought and adherents, and each reaffirmed by more contemporary writers, columnists, and lecturers who presume to beat their drums.

Towering over all the other icons of the Right is the Austrian economist Ludwig von Mises (1881–1973), who started out as a "leftist interventionist but was quickly converted by his study of Carl Menger's *Principles of Economics* (1871) to a self-described libertarian, not a conservative but a liberal in the nineteenth-century sense," according to his biographer, the well-known author and polemicist Murray N. Rothbard.[4] Von Mises's books, published immediately after World War I, were remarkably persuasive; Rothbard noted that they converted "prominent economists and social philosophers out of socialism, including Hayek, the German Wilhelm Röpke, and the Englishman Lionel Robbins."[5] Von Mises is widely considered the most integrative, most scholarly, and most intransigent of conservative economists. Writing in the *Encyclopedia of American Conservatism*, Rothbard summarizes crisply what von Mises concluded:

> The only viable economic policy for the human race was a policy of unrestricted laissez-faire, of free markets and the unhampered exercise of the right of private property, with government strictly limited to the defense of person and property within its territorial area. For Mises was able to demonstrate (a) that the expansion of free markets, the division of labor, and private capital investment is the only possible path to the prosperity and flourishing of the

human race; (b) that socialism would be disastrous for a modern economy because the absence of private ownership of land and capital goods prevents any sort of rational pricing, or estimate of costs, and (c) that government intervention, in addition to hampering and crippling the market, would prove counter-productive and cumulative, leading inevitably to socialism unless the entire tissue of interventions was repealed.[6]

Misesian economics required a noninflationary gold standard and opposition to inflationary bank credit encouraged by central banks. Moving to the United States after World War II, he published what many considered his greatest work, *Human Action* (1949). After his death, the Ludwig von Mises Institute in Auburn, Alabama, opened in 1982. Through its doors have passed thousands of students taught by hundreds of faculty members, who have published over 150 books and monographs, ranging widely in subject, as the titles of two of its more important books reveal: *The Costs of War* (1997) and *Reassessing the Presidency* (2001). Institutes and centers of Misesian economics and social philosophy operate in a dozen major cities on three continents, including Beijing and Moscow.

Arguably the most significant disciple of von Mises, given his influential writings and high-level participation in German free market policies and political structures after World War II, was Wilhelm Röpke. According to the von Mises Institute, he "was able to maintain in one coherent project the best of the logical rigor of Ludwig von Mises, the social understanding of Friedrich Hayek, the anticommunism of Frank Meyer, and the conservative temper of Russell Kirk." Having "devoted his career to combating collectivism in economic, social and political theory," he was operationally grounded in the empirical reality of the political economy.[7] The Misesian Röpke expressed these often forgotten but memorable thoughts: "The highest interests of the community and the indispensable things of life have no exchange value and are negligent if supply and demand are allowed to dominate the field. The supporters of the market do it the worst service by not observing its limits and conditions."[8]

Comparing Contemporary Reality-Starved Conservatives to the Robust Ones of Yore

My reading through a mass of materials of conservative thought, debate, disciplines, and apostates leads me to dispute the contentions of some liberal leaders that dogmatic thinking is what trademarks overall conservative thinking. Or that conservatism is really the only way to justify or rationalize the rule of the rich over the masses.

It is true that contemporary conservatives often ask for this caricature, so maddening is their clinging to rigid abstractions and distancing themselves from facts and realities. For example, their arguments against basic health and safety regulation and its benefits have been delivered with general bombast about the value of free markets and the dangers of socialism. Recently, that approach was taken to the limit by think tanks, which in their discussions fortified an empirically starved plausibility with baseless declarations, rigged costs, and ignored benefits—sometimes to such a heightened degree that it embarrassed their corporate chieftains, who, after all, have accepted and profited from safety devices, such as seat belts, air bags, workplace detection of hazards, and emergency equipment. To paraphrase George Carlin, these think tankers have turned Adam Smith's "invisible hand" into a middle finger.[9]

Consider, by contrast, some of the views of the conservative icons often cited as unbeatable authorities for laissez-faire economies. Friedrich Hayek, a leader of the Austrian School of Economics, argued that the government may need to provide "a comprehensive system of social insurance" to protect the people from "the common hazards of life," including illness.[10] He also conceded that, in a situation of chronic unemployment, the government could have a planning role. In short, he was not an absolutist. Though most known for his deep distaste for state economic planning—whether socialist or communist—and for his belief in its inevitable failure, he was rigorously critical of cartels, monopolies, and anything that smelled of impositional planning or coercion by concentrated corporate power over free markets. One would never sense the existence of these nuanced views listening to modern, clenched-teethed libertarians, who shower Hayek with their accolades as the categorical authority for their strict positions.

"Coercion" of any kind animated libertarian Frank Meyer's writings as well. He wrote that "the only equality premised from the freedom of the person is the equal right of all men to be free from coercion exercised against their life, liberty and prosperity."[11] Russell Kirk was more sensitive to private coercion when he wrote that the true freedom of the person "subsists in community." Kirk, who was a major figure in reviving postwar conservative thought with his seminal book *The Conservative Mind*, pointed to the destructive effect of the imperious auto/highway lobby on communities and mores. He believed that free, self-reliant communities shielded and advanced individual freedom from both statist and private authoritarians. Meyer and Kirk fought over and never reconciled their differences concerning the dangers of coercion, but their followers blithely ignore these qualified thoughts in their polemics against liberals.[12]

When Peter Viereck published his *Conservatism Revisited* in 1950, the liberal Left was preeminent, and "conservatism" signaled militant anticommunism, a strong military, less government, free market economics, and according the benefit of most doubts to the business classes. Viereck did not harp on these themes but felt the key tenet of conservatism was to "root the masses in the universals of civilization."[13] In his view, values precede politics, here recalling Edmund Burke, who was anything but a "rootless doctrinaire." Burke wrote in 1790 that "a state without the means of some change is without the means of its conservation."[14] Viereck made himself unpopular among old-guard Republicans by supporting the rights of workers to form trade unions (and thereby, he added, form nurturing communities) and by backing some New Deal reforms. He excoriated liberals on many scores, however, for their governmental overreach and for other sins that undermine individual initiatives. That did not matter to his harsh conservative critics, who derided this avowed Edmund Burke/John Adams conservative as really a liberal at heart. After all, anticommunist Viereck opposed Joe McCarthy's tactics.

And so it goes with conservatives fighting among themselves. There are plenty of philosophical disagreements, and sometimes turf wars and petty conflicts, between self-described conservatives or libertarians, who classify, slice, and dice their differences in raging polemics in their books, magazines, and pamphlets and now on their websites and blogs.

The Many Messages of Contemporary Conservatives

Here are some samples of their contesting nomenclatures: conservative, paleoconservative, traditional conservative, market conservative, libertarian conservative, libertarian populist, populist conservative, Burkean conservative, Buckley conservative, Kirk conservative, Eisenhower conservative, Goldwater and Reagan conservative, neoconservative, even classical liberal as being today's conservative. Had enough? Try these contemporary micro-distinctions made by today's conservative columnists: David Brooks of the *New York Times* talks about communitarian conservatives as compared with market conservatives; Michael Gerson of the *Washington Post* slices conservatism between "reform conservatism" and "rejectionist conservatism."[15] To further blur public impressions of conservatives, right-wing pollster and wordsmith Frank Luntz unloaded in the April 2012 *Washington Post* on what he called "Myths

About Conservative Voters." The *myths*, he writes, are that they care most about the size of government, want to deport "illegal" immigrants, worship Wall Street, want to slash Social Security and Medicare, and don't care about inequality.[16]

Even top conservative opinion makers sometimes shake the standard mythology. Arch-corporatist right-winger and Mellon heir, billionaire Richard Scaife has been a major factor in building right-wing think tanks, like the Heritage Foundation, and bankrolling right-wing corporatist candidates. That did not stop him from placing a costly, full-page ad in the *Wall Street Journal* in 2011 defending Planned Parenthood and praising founder Margaret Sanger with these words: "I respected her dedication to making health care and birth-control services available to all Americans, especially those with low incomes, no insurance and no other recourse to medical services."[17]

In a vigorous rebuttal of a column by the right-wing George Will, former leading Republican senator Alan Simpson stated he favors campaign finance reform. He even assailed the Republican justices' 5–4 Supreme Court decision in *Citizens United* that said corporations were "persons" for the purpose of letting them make unlimited independent donations for or against any candidates for public office. He took the justices to task for "asserting a remarkable right of corporate personhood that I have yet to find in the Constitution." This is the same Alan Simpson who has ridiculed elderly people, the AARP, and the "entitlements" senior citizens receive.[18]

Flying in the face of conservatives' belief in fiscal responsibility, Republican leaders John Boehner in the House and Mitch McConnell in the Senate routinely oppose any cuts in the giant military budget, no matter how wasteful, redundant, or even unauditable is the spending, and they will sometimes try to give the Pentagon more than it requests. All this for a "U.S. Defense establishment" that author Fareed Zakaria calls "the world's largest socialist economy."[19]

Here are two other examples. Conservative Stanford professor Ronald McKinnon wrote an article for the *Wall Street Journal* called "The Conservative Case for a Wealth Tax."[20] Federal judge J. Harvie Wilkinson III, seen as a paragon of judicial conservatism, wrote a book, *Cosmic Constitutional Theory: Why Americans Are Losing Their Inalienable Right to Self-Governance* (2012), in which he took on both Left and Right constitutional theories. Jeffrey Rosen's review of Wilkinson's book notes "For law students and citizens who are frustrated with the way that all the constitutional methodologies fail, in practice, to deliver on their promise of helping judges separate their political views and judicial decisions, Wilkinson's primer offers a diagnosis of the problem and a self-effacing solution."[21] Take that, Justice Scalia.

In other countries, what self-described conservatives stand for is even more ambiguous and often grounded in pragmatism. In Western Europe, conservative parties generally continued broad-gauged social welfare policies when they defeated and replaced the governing social democratic parties, at least until the recent turbulent recession. The *Times'* David Brooks visited the conservative government in the United Kingdom in May 2011 and pronounced that Prime Minister David Cameron's "Big Society" program "seeks to nurture community bonds, civic activism and social capital, reacting to the concentrated corporate power that weakens the network of entrepreneurs and tradesmen."[22] Maybe these were just words, but lip service is the first step toward acceptance.

David Brooks categorizes the different Washington Republicans as the "beltway bandits," "the show horses," "the big government blowhards," and the "permanent campaigners." "All these groups," he writes, "share the same mentality. They do not see politics as the art of the possible." He called for a fifth category of "practical conservatives."[23]

(He failed to pinpoint another category in the conservative camp, those—regularly politicians—who mouth the slogans of conservatism but violate them in practice. This is where legislators say no to government handouts and yet take the dough. This is where we might place Representative Michele Bachmann, who was presenting herself as a no-holds-barred opponent of government spending and taxation at the same time as her family's farm received $260,000 in subsidies from the Department of Agriculture between 1995 and 2009.[24])

President Reagan's budget chief, conservative David Stockman, recently wrote a book about the "corruption of capitalism in America," denouncing rampant Wall Street speculation, greed, and what one reviewer described as "sweetheart deals between government and industry"—often with the energy sector—driven by corporate lobbyists.[25]

Another George Will column found fault with conservative politicians. Will tore into Senators John McCain and Lindsay Graham in relation to the US attack, with other NATO countries, on Libya. For good measure, he added another column on "Obama's Lawless War," noting that many Republican senators supported it without demanding the congressional votes required by the Constitution to declare war and specifically to authorize and appropriate the monies spent on those attacks.[26]

Indeed, because liberal thinkers tend to be more empirical in their worldly assertions and so don't have the abstract quality of much older conservative thought—or at least so it has been over the past century—they are not comparably revered and recalled authority figures, and are not cited as much in serious public dialogue or conversations. This contrast may be changing, as conservatives shift the grounds of their arguments.

When the foggy militaristic writings of the neoconservatives before and after their Bush-Cheney criminal invasion of Iraq are compared with more recent articles in the *American Conservative* magazine, one can see the changeover to descriptions and empirical arguments that attempt to ground themselves in facts and data. *The American Conservative* and one of its founders, Patrick J. Buchanan, have issued the most devastating critiques of the neocons' lust for unlawful wars. It is a compliment to this magazine that its definition of conservatism, without the need for a qualifying adjective, demonstrates the possibility of Left-Right fusion. Until the recent change in publishers at the *American Conservative*, the *Nation* magazine could easily carry many of its articles without skipping a paragraph.

The divide between the still influential neocons—allied with the preferred politics of the military-industrial complex and the domestic pro-Israeli government lobby—and the traditional conservatives is far wider and harsher than any differences they have with influential corporate liberals or neoliberals. The two conservative camps differ over foreign and military policy, empire, trade agreements, presidential power and constitutional compliance, congressional checks and balances, immigration, the PATRIOT Act, corporate crime and corporate welfare, and the immense powers of Wall Street and its corporate state in Washington, DC.

Writing as a traditional conservative, Buchanan, in his 2004 book *Where the Right Went Wrong: How Neoconservatives Subverted the Reagan Revolution and Hijacked the Bush Presidency*, hurls thickets of historical fact against the neocons' myths, lies, and hypocrisies, which they garnish with a belief in militaristic, patriotic exceptionalism, touting America's leaders' inherent humanism, a faith belied by the deliberate slaughter of civilians in the United States during the Civil War and the mass incinerations over Dresden and Tokyo, Hiroshima and Nagasaki during World War II, whose purpose was to "terrorize the population," to use the language of our leaders at the time.[27]

It is too bad C-SPAN could not sponsor debates between the likes of Buchanan and the armchair, draft-exempted belligerents Dick Cheney, Richard Perle, Paul Wolfowitz, and Elliott Abrams. Such an exchange would have destroyed the liberal's monocultural stereotype of conservatives for a long time.

Another case of confusing conservatives of different stripes appeared when Representative Dennis Kucinich, the active progressive, insisted to the *Washington Post* that his proposed Department of Peace "is actually a conservative position. Peace is becoming the conservative position. By not getting into military conflicts, we conserve lives, we conserve America's resources, we conserve America's money."[28] The former Ohio lawmaker, if he stopped relying on his dictionary definition of traditional conservation, would not find many militaristic Republican "conservatives" in Congress concurring with him.

Of course, part of the problem of the confusion among conservatives is that almost everyone is calling themselves, in some policy arenas, a conservative these days. Consider how times have changed. In the early fifties Peter Viereck quoted liberal Robert Bendiner: "Out of some 140,000,000 people in the United States, at least 139,500,000 are liberals, to hear them tell it. . . . Rare is the citizen who can bring himself to say, 'Sure I'm a conservative.' . . . Any American would sooner drop dead than proclaim himself a reactionary."[29] Nowadays, the situation is more the reverse.

But since, as we have seen, it's getting hard to tell what a conservative is, with so many of them adopting liberal, even radical positions, we might wonder how different at least the traditional conservative is from those holding classical liberal views.

After all, both conservatives and liberals claim the US Constitution and the Declaration of Independence authoritatively and generically embody their principles and philosophy, not just their sense of patriotism.

What About the Voters?

Now let's go find out how people on Main Street answer the questions of what is a liberal and what is a conservative. After all, intellectuals can battle their respective adversaries inside and outside their spheres of thought, making rarified distinctions, but the votes come from the people, who attach images and steadfast behaviors to those two labels. Whatever names they choose, people love to label themselves and others politically. It is convenient shorthand, designating one's beliefs and providing a sense of belonging. Here the labels do not come with the micro slicing and dicing of the intelligentsia.

Most Americans who call themselves libertarians or conservative are, like most self-styled liberals, largely politically inactive. As noted, half of either camp do not even vote. So what are they thinking when they apply these labels to their identities?

Here are some unsurprising replies received from questions I've asked regular people in conversations around the country.

- "I'm a conservative because I want lower taxes."
- "I'm a conservative because I want less government, less regulation, less Big Brother, less welfare, and a strong military."
- "I'm a religious conservative because I want to see strong family values respected. I am against abortion."
- "I'm a conservative because I believe in the free enterprise system, not socialism. I want to vote for candidates who are tough on crime and support the right to bear arms."
- "I'm a conservative because I don't believe we're as smart as our ancestors and their tested traditions."
- "I'm a conservative because the liberals have ruined our country with wasteful government programs and overregulation, and have always been soft on atheistic communism."

Now what does a proud liberal say in similar chats at the proverbial diner?

- "I'm a liberal because I'm tired of seeing the little guy, the working stiff, get screwed by the big boys."
- "I'm a liberal because my elderly parents would be out on the streets if they didn't have Social Security and Medicare. Caring for others in need is being a liberal."
- "I'm a liberal because as a minority who's felt discrimination, I know tolerance is a good thing for everybody. The civil rights laws were pushed by liberals and were long overdue."

- "I'm a liberal because I don't want the rich messing with our elections and right-wingers telling us how to behave and who to associate with. There's a reason for the separation of state and religion."
- "I'm a liberal because liberal philosophy is a fairness philosophy. Also, I favor Main Street over Wall Street, which always gets the bailouts."
- "I want my children to drink clean water, breathe clean air, and eat safe food. You can say I'm an environmentalist. I suppose that's liberal."

(I'm sure you can add other reasons to both lists.)

What can be said about such identifications? First, they reflect the constant hammering of these same associations by the politicians and allied radio and TV talk show hosts year after year. Second, they probably flow from experiences such as a run-in with the IRS, dealing with some irritating regulations, being blocked from school prayer, seeing the flag disrespected, getting sick or ripped off, being raised in a family that deeply empathized with the poor or being poor, and being African American, Hispanic, or a woman subject to racist or sexist discrimination. The pluses and minuses felt in life quickly fortify the images that attach to the "conservative" or "liberal" label. An identifier with one camp or the other could be part of a conservative, evangelical church or a member of a union or military family. They could be hereditary Republican or Democratic voters because of their grandparents and parents, and therefore they are self-styled as either conservatives or liberals.

The Danger of Looking Solely at Labels

When citizens engage in one-step conclusions about the meaning of liberalism or conservatism and don't engage in the complexity of these traditions, they put themselves at risk of being unable to detect the hypocrisy of the leaders of their own camp and fail to confront their false and misleading statements. Sometimes, even when they learn that a so-called conservative politician has violated nearly every principle of conservatism, the voter is so mesmerized by the hype that the realities of the situation are ignored.

For example, here is an exchange I had years ago with an avid Ronald Reagan fan:

"Why are you such a Reagan supporter?"
"Simple: he is for lower taxes, less regulation, less spending, and smaller government."
"Well, did you know that he increased the federal debt more in sheer dollars than all previous presidents combined, from George Washington through Jimmy Carter? He sent all his deficit-spending budgets to Congress from the get-go."
"Is that so?"
"Did you know that he raised taxes fifteen times after he lowered them in 1981–1982?"
"No. That's hard to believe."
"Did you know that in January 1989 he left government larger in number of employees and contractors than he received from Jimmy Carter? And did you also know that before he was president, he would speak out against government subsidies to businesses, but as president he continued and even increased some of them?"
"Are these really the facts?"
"Yes. Are you still a Reagan backer?"
"Forever."

How Progressives Can Change Minds and How Politicians Befuddle Them

The previous example indicates that it's difficult to budge the opinion of someone who has become fixated on political labels. When it comes to dealing with self-designated political categories, altering an individual's opinion is, as Professor Howard Gardner points out in his challenging book *Changing Minds*, quite complex and difficult.[30] Presidential political campaigns focus on changing the minds of maybe 10 percent of the electorate. The vast number of remaining voters do not waver. Most voters vote the party, regardless of the candidate, even though they say they vote for the candidate.

The key to opening people's minds on matters of specific public import is to go down the abstraction ladder. While categorical positioning is strong at the aforementioned higher levels of generalization and labels, going down to situations where people live, work, buy, eat, raise their children, and play invites a different kind of thinking—one that reflects people's sense of fairness, their desire for health and safety, their inherent fondness for the harmonious wisdom that often was called "plain old common sense."

Take, for example, people who do not like government regulation. Ask them whether they want their cars recalled for correction when the manufacturer discovers a deadly defect? Obviously, they say, "Sure." Then ask, if the manufacturer doesn't do this, whether the Department of Transportation should have the regulatory authority to make them recall the vehicles? The same sequence can be followed with government safety regulation on medicines, drinking water, air pollution, workplace dangers, electrical wiring, and other, often silent, invisible perils to one's health and safety. Granted, there will be, at even more concrete levels, disagreements on how far to go with safety standards or penalties, but still, support for these regulations' existence clearly embraces all but the hardest-core libertarians, who believe that if people want to avoid air pollution, they should just move away or not inhale. However, for most people, when dogma meets life's perceived necessities, the latter usually wins the polls.

Even the charming, soft-spoken Ronald Reagan ran up a hill when he faced the public's rejection of the judgment he made from the top of the abstraction ladder. Campaigning for president in 1980 in Michigan, he attacked the proposed air bag standard as restricting our freedom. I sort of agreed with him. Upon being asked for comment by a Detroit reporter, I said, "Yes, the air bag does restrict the driver's and passenger's freedom to go through the windshield in a crash."

The time-tested approach by the few who wish to politically dominate the many is to pull the many up the abstraction ladder, away from the realities on the ground into the stratosphere of general principles, values, symbols, myths, and particularly images, whether these are secular or selective religious references. Republicans and their wealthy backers have courted and assisted the Pentecostals and fundamentalists. The Democrats and their operatives, on the other hand, welcomed the social gospel of mainline Protestant churches in the struggles for civil rights, peace, and improvement of the plight of the poor. Since the sixties, the language of religion in political rallies and elections has intensified. This is especially the case for the Republicans, who kept up the abstractions as they focused on hot-button issues such as abortion and the danger of ungodly gays. (Yet down at the family level, away from the abstractions, Dick Cheney gives unconditional love to his lesbian daughter.) At the same time, the Democrats, recognizing some distance between formal religious institutions and political events, have stayed more focused on the widely felt deprivations of the people, tying this issue in less strongly with religion.

Along with the strategy of arguing from the top of the abstraction ladder, another ruse to confuse the people is the presentation of a bipolar view of liberals and conservatives as totally distinctive, a perspective fed by numerous false stereotypes, which service the controlling processes of the ruling classes. It is a sophisticated strategy of divide and rule put forward by the governing monetized elite, who watch it work like magic to distract voters, along with the mainstream media, both during and between elections, into seeing the world divided into two irreconcilable camps. Few note the points I have raised here, such as the divisions within conservatism as well as the confluence of many liberal and conservative positions. Instead, by focusing on the battle between the two camps, everyone overlooks the fact that the motor of our whole system is the workings of concentrated power, which is abusing the vast majority of the people indiscriminately. This "imaginary" division is promulgated even in elementary school education, where, for example, *Scholastic News* class materials instruct millions of schoolchildren to choose one of only two sides for mock elections.

Where a clear mind will note the distinctions and confluences I have outlined in this chapter, corporatism is by far the greatest practical generator for perpetuating and funding the belief in this rigid, distracting divide.

3

Hands Reach Across the Aisle, Though Often Slapped Back by Wily Corporatists

Hands Across the Great Divide

The frequency of liberal/conservative cosponsorship of legislation on Capitol Hill is greater than most people realize. Few of these alliances go anywhere, but it's a start for breaking the ice. The far more visible battles between intransigent leaders of the two parties give the impression of top-down, complete polarization—a word used with numbing repetition in recent years. But on any day one can check the pending legislation in Congress and find many bills with the conservative/liberal imprimatur. Senator Ron Wyden (D-OR) is probably the most attracted to finding a Republican or two and putting bills into this bipartisan hopper. For these efforts he receives some publicity—as with his bipartisan health insurance plan—unlike other lawmakers, whose placements are mostly ignored. In 2013, Senator Wyden teamed up with Republican senator Rand Paul to introduce legislation that would legalize industrial hemp grown in the United States, and he united with Republican senator Lisa Murkowski to require disclosure of donors giving over $1,000 to any organization engaged in federal political activity.

These major Left-Right initiatives cover lots of territory, but few reach the committee hearing stage, still fewer ever reach the House or Senate floor, and almost none are enacted as free-standing legislation, in contrast to minor amendments (or earmarks) inserted in "must-pass" larger bills, such as appropriations for the military budget.

One rare major success was the campaign finance bill passed in 2003, which is called the McCain-Feingold Act after Senator John McCain (R-AZ) and Senator Russ Feingold (D-WI). In his 2000 presidential campaign, Senator McCain repeatedly tore into big money in politics. The LC sponsorship was essential to the bill's success, helping the sponsors negotiate the grueling process of fending off business lobbyists and also key in amending the bill on its way to passage.

At the outset, it should be noted that many bills pass with bipartisan support of varying degrees, especially on the final vote prior to passage. These include the major appropriation bills for the departments, such as Defense, Treasury, Agriculture, Commerce, and the like. More controversial bills also have passed this way, including the periodic giant allocations of taxpayer dollars to the Iraq and Afghan wars. Also in this category of bipartisan support are appropriations for the International Monetary Fund and, recently, for the renewal of the Export-Import Bank, which finances foreign purchases of US exports such as Boeing's aircraft. Bipartisanship tends to jell repeatedly when business interests make clear their demands, backing them up by the usual campaign donations and other lobbying techniques.

Why These Hands Seldom Clasp Victory

Apart from those powerful unifying bonds and moments of coalition, convergent legislation passing simply because it's the right thing to do is not very likely. One obstacle is that the leadership in the House and Senate tend to lock horns over contentious issues—often historical or ideological ones—that are primed to hold their base and garner election-time advantage. If the legislators are in the midst of fighting over Obamacare, renewals of the Bush tax cuts, Social Security changes, abortion rights, and environmental regulations, they are not in any frame of mind to make each other look good through collaborative support of other bills that may well bring advantages to the public but may also lead to congressional or White House complications or unhappy consequences down the road. This is the case even with relatively straightforward efforts to reassert the constitutional or institutional role of Congress in foreign and military affairs vis-à-vis the White House.

Here's a case in point. In 2011, Democrat Dennis Kucinich and Republican Walter Jones introduced legislation to amend the War Powers Act to strengthen congressional oversight. It was directed at an increasing executive branch overreach in using military force that was a common hallmark of both the Bush and the Obama administrations. As such, the proposed law strove to restore some of the checks and balances of our federal system. The bill received no public hearings, even though its thrust would have received broad support in any private poll of members of Congress.

In a similar move in 2012, Jones and James McGovern, a strong progressive Massachusetts Democrat, teamed up for H.C. Res. 107, declaring it to be the sense of Congress that a president who initiates war without the express authorization of Congress is involved in "high crimes and misdemeanors" within the meaning of Article 2, section 4, of the Constitution.[1] This resolution is not a minor one for a Congress that needs to be reminded about the Constitution's Article 1, section 8—that the war-declaration authority is reserved exclusively for Congress. The last war Congress declared was in December 1941 against Japan and Germany.[2] There have been numerous undeclared wars of choice by the United States since then.

Both the legislation and the resolution have been completely ignored by the leadership of the two parties who gave strong signals to their flocks to remain silent. Why risk giving the other party any chips? Why pile more issues on busy desks? Why raise and rally public awareness of congressional abdication, which might well lead to citizens calling on legislators to assume more constitutional responsibility for military and foreign policies, practices, and mishaps? Let "mum" be the word.

Further, there are no outside pressure groups on these issues, as there are with the corporate-connected neocons, who have pushed Congress and the White House for military aggressiveness by a unilaterally deciding presidency. Just the opposite is the case. Jones, McGovern, and Kucinich were unable to call on much of an organized outside support structure, which would have the requisite muscle to get things moving on Capitol Hill. Bereft of any news coverage and unable to obtain any mass media access, let alone any commentary whatsoever from the presidential bully pulpit, they could not expect many people back home to mobilize behind their case, of which most were unaware.

Establishing Laws Against Corporate Welfare Where Hands Should Have Joined But Didn't

This stagnant environment blocks even more vibrant causes from acquiring any momentum. In 1998, the time seemed finally ripe to push the legislative envelope and demand some curtailment of the massive bustling bazaar of accounts receivables, government tax breaks, and payouts to businesses, which years earlier I labeled "corporate welfare." Just about every large company was on the government dole—including foreign firms operating in the United States. After all, there were hundreds of such giveaways. Signs indicated that the potential for such legislation met the preliminary criteria for convergence. Condemned in reports by such influential right-of-center think tanks as the Heritage Foundation and the Cato Institute as well as by the Progressive Policy Institute, Common Cause, and Public Citizen, "corporate welfare" and, its right-wing name, "crony capitalism" became dirty words. Numerous exposés by CBS's *Sixty Minutes,* ABC's *It's Your Money,* the *Washington Post,* the *New York Times,* the *Wall Street Journal, Time* magazine and the Associated Press year after year began to seep into the political consciousness and even put the dirty words in the vernacular of more and more of the public. Scandals and greed regarding corporate subsidies, giveaways of the public's natural resources and technology transfers, abuse of eminent domain to benefit large companies, and ever larger bailouts angered both conservatives and liberals—for both similar and different reasons.

Conservatives believed it was unfair to taxpayers that crony capitalism distorted free markets, picking winners as industrial policy, rather than as a result of market forces; hurt small business; and corrupted the arm's-length relationship they viewed as proper between business and government. Liberals saw corporate welfare as giving away taxpayer money and the commons on the public lands—minerals, forests—in favor of big oil and coal over renewable and conserving energy technologies; hurting the small farmer; weakening regulatory policies; and generally giving away valuable public assets, such as government research and development findings, for free without any payment or conditions in the public interest. There was also a genuine overlap of concurrence between each side's rationales.

It was clear that some powerful members of Congress, though not at the top leadership level, were using conservative doctrine to attack corporatist positions that favored the myriad corporate welfare programs—so numerous, in fact, there was no comprehensive compilation of them anywhere in the federal government. One of these legislators was the current Ohio governor, Republican John Kasich, then chair of the House Budget Committee and a close ally of Newt Gingrich in the latter's rise to the Speakership. In 1999, I proposed to Kasich that he hold the first public hearing on corporate welfare in American history—looking at not just one program but going across the whole continuum. I would recommend to him a number of substantial witnesses on both sides of the ideological divide, naming Grover Norquist of Americans for Tax Reform and Robert McIntyre of Citizens for Tax Justice as examples. After some weeks, during which he probably was testing the permissible waters—already he had made rare waves in Republican circles by declaring the military budget to be bloated and suitable for cutting—he gave the green light.

The Budget Committee hearing took the better part of the day (June 30, 1999) and should have created a minor sensation. However, the media generally ignored or downplayed it, in part because, while the corporate lobbyists kept an eye on the proceedings, they stayed quiet, holding back on any opposition until they saw signs that an actual piece of legislation might come out of the deliberations from Kasich. Lobbyists have sensitive antennae when it comes to gauging just how committed a committee chair is to pushing his or her hearing toward action. They read Kasich as wanting to display his principled stand as a conservative and going no further. His opening statement, while courteous and receptive, gave as his major concern the unfair competition that corporate welfare, usually wrung from the government by Big Business, inflicts on small business. Kasich also knew that Heritage, Cato, and others were doing the same thing—burnishing their pure marketplace conservative credentials, but not actually pressing for action on Capitol Hill, which would have troubled their wealthy, freeloading funders. The smaller-budgeted Progressive Policy Institute and Common Cause, clearly against these corporate freebies, simply had no resources to give their views any sustained political cutting edge. No candidates, whether incumbents or challengers, had run on a promise to end corporate welfare "as we know it," as they assuredly did with poverty welfare disbursements.

Even though the LibCons put forth at the Kasich hearing their first-stage priority list of corporate welfare programs for elimination, there was no pickup.

In theory, as a general agenda for LC convergence, direct and indirect taxpayer subsidies to fat-cat corporations, ones that are overpaying their bosses and underpaying their shareholder dividends while often not performing in return for the subsidizers' intents—e.g., synthetic fuels and improved auto engine efficiency—would be hard to surpass. In practice, it didn't seem to matter, even though, from time to time, a Democrat and a Republican would jointly introduce a bill to rid the country of an especially egregious subsidy or giveaway. There was just no traction to rid America of the curse of "aid to dependent corporations," to borrow a phrase from the social welfare world. It didn't matter that lawmakers told their various publics how much they abstractly believed in limited government, fiscal responsibility, and accountability to the taxpayers, because they then turned around and unfurled a flurry of annual votes backing the corporate freeloaders. A few shameless lawmakers, such as Rep. Michele Bachmann, even had their own businesses that received various federal payouts. Importantly, as happened in relation to the law and the resolution on presidential war powers, no one in Congress, from either party, felt any push, heat, or encouragement from the White House or the media to change this status quo that keeps Washington busier with handing out largesse to corporations than with any other regular engagements. The process of Washington saving Wall Street years later in 2008–2009 reflected this institutionalization of the corporate state or what some call "corporate socialism." Given how millions of Americans suffered from job losses, home foreclosures, greater consumer debt, and taxpayer debt on their children, how apt was Gore Vidal's expression that America "is a unique society where you have free enterprise for the poor and socialism for the rich."[3]

During a debate with Ronald Reagan in 1977, sponsored by the American Enterprise Institute, I elicited from him a clear distaste for government propping up business. He noted that he kept telling his corporate friends not to have their hands in Washington's trough. He cited as an example of an unwarranted corporate giveaway the Jones Act, which restricted US port-to-port shipping to US-flag ships, thereby keeping shipping rates high. Reagan was known as a rhetorical opponent of business policies that begin and end with taxpayers holding the bag—another way of keeping taxes higher. Yet, on becoming president in 1981, Mr. Reagan continued and amplified corporate welfare, and avoided bringing up the topic in any of his speeches

Corporations Block Bipartisan Hand Clasping

Many other convergences suffer similar fates when liberals and conservatives join together only to find that, though they may be in a numerical majority, they are blocked by commercial interests. In 2003, the FCC voted 3–2 to allow even greater concentration of ownership by Big Media over television, radio, and newspaper properties in any community, in spite of an avalanche of protest by Americans of all persuasions, from the NRA to Common Cause. The battle moved to Congress. In an astonishingly lopsided result, the House voted 400–21, for the first time in its history overturning an FCC decision and handing Big Media a stunning defeat. Yet Big Media recovered and stanched a rising swell in the Senate, whose members were also responding to tens of thousands of emails and other messages from the voters back home. Unfortunately, the conflict was drawn out. Unlike corporations, the people had no staying power, and the controversy faded away. The FCC decision survived.

In the summer of 2010, a most unlikely group of politicians gathered a group of experts spanning the ideological spectrum whose charge was to reduce the military budget. The conveners, Representatives Ron Paul and Barney Frank, were not lonely outliers.

And a majority of Congress silently supported their effort, being well informed about military financial profligacy, which has been regularly documented by the investigative arm of the Congress, the Government Accountability Office, in report after report on the waste, fraud, and duplication that absorbs huge amounts of money. Pentagon contractor fraud, theft, huge cost overruns, and defects, also pointed out by public Pentagon audits, are old news to members of Congress. They know all about it, but they are not about to openly take on the powerful "military-industrial complex" about which President Eisenhower warned. Even moving against obsolete or redundant weapons systems or yet another aircraft carrier or submarine, which would seem natural following the end of the Soviet Union, and which even retired generals and admirals have called for, has proven to be too much for these politicians. Too much campaign cash, too much economic muscle in their districts, often backed by labor unions, which see such contracts as jobs programs, are weighed in the balance. Taxpayers are still paying massive billions of dollars for the ill-advised F-22, the troubled Osprey helicopter, the skyrocketing costs of the F-35, which continue to be in production at a time when their purpose—countering the Soviet Union—is no more. So, again, the task force's findings came to nothing.[4]

In 2010, a grand alliance of conservatives and liberals organized around expanding the whistle-blowing rights and remedies of federal government employees. The bipartisan appeal of this legislation made it about as invulnerable to attack as any bill in modern congressional history. After all, who could oppose assuring protections for courageous public servants who want to expose fraud, waste, and corruption mostly by corporate contractors on the government? Well, for a start, the many companies and consulting firms, such as Raytheon, Lockheed Martin, CACI, and Booz Allen Hamilton, that benefit from federal employees who facilitate corrupt practices. Then there are the members of the executive branch who look to these companies for future jobs. But this time these vested interests couldn't really go public. They worked behind the scenes to dilute provisions of the bill, but they could not seriously gut it. At the very end of the session, Republican and Democrat sponsors (Senators Burris, Cardin, Carper, Collins, Grassley, Leahy, Levin, Lieberman, Mikulski, Pryor, Tester, and Voinovich) and their supporters, most prominently the whistle-blower-defending Government Accountability Project, were figuratively ready to break open the champagne bottles.[5] Suddenly, they learned that a secret hold had been put on the bill by two undisclosed senators, as the paralyzing Senate rules permitted. The bill died in the Senate. S. 372 would probably have received a 90 percent approval by the American people if it could have been put to a vote. But President Obama did sign a similar bill (S. 743), which finally passed in 2012, when time overcame the effect of last-ditch holds, who turned out to have been Republican senators Jon Kyl (R-AZ) and Jeff Sessions (R-AL).

Commercial interests do not tolerate federal study commissions either, even when proposed by members of both parties in Congress, if there is any chance they will be shining light on their business practices. In 2002, Senator John McCain introduced a bill to establish a federal commission on corporate welfare (S. 2181: Corporate Subsidy Reform Commission Act). The reaction was swift by the corporate welfare kings working behind the scenes. It never received a hearing, nor did he reintroduce it during the next session, although his bipartisan charge related intimately to the then-urgent debate on deficits and taxes. The Arizona senator has never reintroduced this sensible measure.

In another example, Democratic senator Jim Webb introduced S. 306 to establish a National Criminal Justice Commission on prison reforms, a subject long overdue for consideration. Again, though attracting supporters from both sides of the aisle, it has not even been given a Senate hearing. The prison-industrial complex, including its union backers, made sure that the bill withered on the vine, blocking Senator Webb's move. Again, were it put to a private vote in Congress, the yeas would have carried.

It might be asked: If there are majorities in favor of these varied measures, how can lobbies block these initiatives from even leaving the gate or not making that one last step before expected victory? The answer can be called "the Khyber Pass block strategy." Corporatists know in amazing detail where and when the various bottlenecks (Khyber Passes) afford the opportunity to stop the actions of even a great majority of senators. They know the procedures, the timing, the tight schedules, the personalities, the stealth moves to make. The mere threat of a filibuster is enough to get the Senate majority leader to not take the bill to the floor for debate. And always lurking is the campaign money given, withheld, or awarded to a primary challenger. After all, as the Oklahoma sage Will Rogers said eighty years ago: "Congress is the best money can buy."

When Hands Have Met

Consider, on the other hand, the convergence that did come about to advance air bag installation in motor vehicles at a moment when the contact point for action—a government procurement agency—was beyond the auto industries' lobbying clutches. In 1985, frustrated with the auto companies blocking the Department of Transportation from issuing a mandatory air bag standard for motor vehicles, I decided to do an end run by going through the government procurement process. I knew that through the General Services Administration (GSA), its purchasing arm, the federal government bought over forty thousand new cars a year for its federal employees. Taking the motto "The customer is always right" down to the GSA's chief, Gerald Carmen, an arch antiregulatory New Hampshire conservative, I made the arguments that he should get air bags in any new cars he bought because it would save lives, save taxpayer money, and establish a large private market for promoting air bags as a result of the stimulus of a government purchase. Carmen eyed me cautiously. I knew he was a former auto parts dealer as well as, in the key New Hampshire primary, an early backer of Ronald Reagan. He was rich and did not need the job. Most importantly, he had no awe of the auto companies, having been a part of a supplementary industry that was not always treated well.

To Carmen, my request was not one for regulation, but one for smart, efficient buying on behalf of the taxpayer. He let Ford, GM, and Chrysler know of GSA's intention to issue specifications for a preliminary buy of five thousand cars with driver-side air bags. GM knew what was in the works and did not like it. At a social gathering, a GM lobbyist came up to Carmen and tried to dissuade him. No dice. One car company, Ford, said they would bid and, being the only bid, won the job to sell and equip five thousand Tempos with the safety system.

What happened next showed that domino effects are not always negative. Chrysler's Lee Iacocca, long a vocal derider of air bags, switched positions and, in a dramatic number of full-page newspaper ads showing his picture, he exclaimed in large bold print: "WHO SAYS YOU CAN'T TEACH AN OLD DOG NEW TRICKS?" He was announcing driver-side air bags as standard equipment on several Chrysler models. It wasn't long before the Department of Transportation finally moved to require air bags for drivers and front-seat passengers as standard equipment on all motor vehicles. Many lives were saved and injuries were prevented.

Carmen had full authority to do what he did, but I'm sure he checked with the White House as a courtesy. He became a believer in using government purchasing as a taxpayer efficiency tool, delivering a major address on the subject. Had I prejudged him according to the stereotype, defining him solely as a very conservative businessman and supporter of Ronald Reagan, my initial trip to GSA would never have occurred. There was common ground between us on this matter, though not on many other policies of the Reagan administration.

Potential Pitfalls on the Route to Convergence

There are many ways to cross the aisle inside and outside of government. The challenge is to root these convergence movements as deeply as possible in common values and solid facts. Outside of government, existing or likely common ground has to become sufficiently visible so that the participants can reach first base, and that means confronting and overcoming some pretty mundane but persistent obstacles.

What transpired before and on February 20, 2010, and thereafter provides an instructive example. On that day in a Washington, DC, hotel, forty persons gathered, all opposed to militarism, wars, and the American empire. To any observer this would seem to be nothing special so far, until they learned that around the large conference table was a multiracial attendance of libertarians, progressives, conservatives, centrists, and radicals—self-described with the usual qualifications—who were going to deliberate for the entire day. The conference was inspired and funded by Republican and former Cold War hawk George D. O'Neill Jr., of Lake Wales, Florida, and coordinated by former Green Party Senate candidate and legal scholar Kevin Zeese.

The meeting participants were outspoken and un-sandpapered. Obviously, those at the table came from a common consensus of what they wanted to stop, and they proceeded to discuss in more detail both the malady and what needed to be done. Many had their own constituency from decades of activism, writing, rallying, and taking their lumps. They included Doug Bandow, Medea Benjamin, Glen Ford, Tom Hayden, Bill Kauffman, William Lind, Daniel McCarthy, Carl Oglesby, Robert Pollin, Cindy Sheehan,

Jeffrey Tayler, Katrina vanden Heuvel, Jesse Walker, Dave Wagner, George Wilson, Thomas E. Woods Jr., and others. Woods spoke of previous Left-Right coalitions against war, including one that involved Andrew Carnegie, who was against the Spanish-American war, while Zeese laid out the components of a detailed "effective antiwar movement."

The gathering met its title, "The Across the Political Spectrum Conference Against War and Militarism," causing Paul Buhle to say that "there never was such a boundary-crossing event before, at least not in my fifty-year political lifetime."[6]

As the hours wore on, some fissures emerged over tactics and on what to do with the huge savings, which would come from cutting military budgets. The savings were an incentive to oppose war making and could also fund a redirecting of our country. The most difficult subject of who, how, and when to mobilize was not expeditiously or functionally considered.

Around three or four PM, people started moving to catch their planes. Few if any volunteered to assume the tasks that would have brought the goals of the meeting to the next step, though email addresses were exchanged. The truth was these were busy people, some of whom were plumb tired and philosophically pessimistic after decades of struggle. Okay, so how much could we expect from one meeting? At its end, I didn't sense that this was a breakout event.

George O'Neill, with assistance from Buhle, Kauffman, and Zeese, gathered together many short, to-the-point articles by the participants and published them in early 2011 under the title of *ComeHomeAmerica.us*.[7] In his note accompanying the copy he sent me, O'Neill related that "we are all working toward a larger and more public conference this year." It never happened.

What did happen? Certainly there was passion; these were not theoretical, armchair philosophers. But their cups were full with what they chose to make their daily work, as was mine. A few went back to nonviolent civil disobedience against America's wars; others displayed their outrage in a variety of individual ways. All seemed busy with their various work and family responsibilities. But their sum (postconference) was less than their parts, which isn't exactly what the participants may have had in mind when they accepted O'Neill's bold invitation.

Making Effective Convergences Happen

Welcome to the world of well-meaning but ultimately nonproductive, secularly ecumenical conferences, especially ones that do not hammer out a proclamation or call to action like the Ripon statement or the Declaration of Independence. What were the problems? First, the conference was too short. It needed to break down into workshops the next day with declared programmatic outcomes, ones that would explore many directions, in many dimensions. One such workshop could have focused on enlisting some thoughtful, generous, super-rich sponsor to provide the essential resources for field organizers, communicators, and grassroots lecturers, creating the type of infrastructure that propelled forward the populist-farmer movement in the 1880s and 1890s, which was so successful.

Think of starting a business, building a trade union, or launching a nonprofit institution, and imagine what efforts have to follow any such convening meeting for the plan to come to fruition.

Initiators who put forces in motion are usually those who commit their time to these objectives, day after day spreading the dynamic and rooting the mission. If the mission is too large for the number of available participants, then a small secretariat needs to be set up that can work to broaden the base beyond that of the founders. This group can tap into focused energies and build up a critical mass of the involved to ready the project for takeoff.

Obviously, disparate motivations will attract different people to support a cause: anything from making money in a new field to resisting felt injustices in the workplace to being driven by a singular vision. That's the point: multiple motivations will drive the joining of unlikely activists in one cause. During preparations for beginning a project, people's motivating passions need to be identified and given opportunities to constructively proliferate so that they cannot easily be discouraged or sidelined by other activities. Of course, for success, some of the proponents have to see the mission as their number 1 commitment.

It helps to propose these preconditions to a successful launch before the first invitations are sent, so that the invitees do not get the impression they are going to a talkfest simply to test their mutual congeniality and attitudes toward the issue. Moreover, there is no substitute for inviting a sizable number of young people, typically filled with vitality and vigor, who may desire to make the goal of the project their life's work. At a get-together like this, wisdom plays when energy avails.

Even a Successful Convergence Can Be Derailed When It Enters the Public Sphere

Another quite different conjoining of Left-Right came out of the conservative American Bar Association (ABA) in 2005–2006 under the leadership of its president, corporate lawyer Michael Greco of Boston. Having been a lapsed member of the staid and cautious ABA, I was astonished at what Greco pulled off. He organized two task forces of lawyers—with the usual philosophical differences—to put out two white papers on the constitutional violations of President George W. Bush in the area of executive overreach of power. Greco and his colleagues then obtained a unanimous endorsement by the ABA's Board of Delegates, comprised of five hundred attorneys, largely business-oriented and Republicans.[8] He did this by the force of his character, with a sense of urgency about high-level White House–led lawlessness, and by bringing together lawyers on the task forces who had worked for the FBI, CIA, and Defense Department as well as lawyers working in the fields of civil liberties and constitutional government. The delegates looked at the roster and identified with some of the names as "people like us," people who are true patriots who believe in our country's commitment to the rule of law over powerful public officials.

The white papers were sent separately at different times to the president and released to the press. They included arrests without charges, illegal surveillance, and rampant signing statements by George W. Bush declaring his power to ignore enforcement of bills signed into law. President George W. Bush did not even have an aide acknowledge receipt and made no comment on the considered judgments of the largest bar association in the world. More remarkably, apart from a short Associated Press report, the mainstream press ignored these declarations on a presidency that was deep in an undeclared war, one getting worse by the month in terms of American casualties and much, much worse in terms of Iraqi casualties, as well as overall destruction and cost.

Whoever the clients were or could be for these ABA attorneys, they put their country and their fealty to the constitution first and foremost. They had no client agenda, no commercial inducement. As officers of the court, they just believed it was the lawful thing to do, regardless of any disfavor they may have received from others in their party, regardless of their social and professional peers, regardless of the usual lucrative inducements awaiting commitments to casuistry. One would think that our country would take notice, ponder, deliberate, and invite these lawyers to conventions, media programs, and state and local bar associations. For the most part, it did not happen. Why was this action derailed?

First, it was not meant to be a budgeted, grassroots movement. So there were no follow-up programs, tours, demands for public hearings, litigation, or networking. The white papers were placed before our society's underdeveloped democratic institutions, which were unprepared to pick up and take to new heights of action anything suggested by their insights. Despite growing polls against the Iraq War, the papers were lost to indifference. Neither the legal profession, nor local political entities, nor civic associations, nor law schools and universities took this precious asset and amplified its impact.

Second, Mr. Greco's presidency was for a one-year term during which he traveled the nation speaking about his concerns. Before returning to his practice in Boston, he told me that his successor informed him she was not going to pick up where he left off. So that luminous expression of exceptional professional duty by the ABA simply faded away. The Iraq War became more violent and led to more serious damage to a society of twenty-five million people who presented no threat to the United States. Meanwhile, in 2009, the US government plunged deeper into another war-quagmire in Afghanistan through similar unconstitutional aggressions.

Obviously *saying* the perceived truth, as did Greco and colleagues, is different from *meaning* it so much you take it to the powers-that-be. That is when the repercussions and retaliations start to kick in. Few have the fortitude to withstand such pressures. Even the heroic Greco has been discouraged and less active since he returned to his Boston law practice.

Convergences on Procedural Issues

When convergence is nipped in the bud, at least we know there was a bud. What happens when members of a potential Left-Right convergence prejudge and completely turn off each other even when there is undeniable agreement on a singular policy, though the sides are divided by a welter of other disagreements? This is how an alliance I formed was judged and condemned by those on my side who wouldn't look beyond the multiple disagreements I had with a controversial political figure to see the one area where we had unity.

One day in 1994 Pat Buchanan and I joined together at a news conference to denounce NAFTA and the proposed World Trade Organization agreement. We had overlapping concerns, such as the enormous override of our sovereignty, courts, agencies, and legislatures by the unelected transnational governments to which the United States signed on with many other countries to constitute these agreements. And we had separate criticisms. For my part, these criticisms were the weakening of health, safety, and environmental regulations to the lowest common denominators that these pacts would endorse. Buchanan didn't much like regulations from any directions.

Some of my associates wondered how I could ally with one of the last devotees of Nixon in the White House. How could I overlook his other positions, which were so regressive and tribalist? In turn, he got calls from his ideological fraternity asking why he was associating with what they called an "antibusiness" or "anticapitalist" adversary. Buchanan would tell them, "Ralph and I have many disagreements, but we want to express them under the rules of the U.S., not the secret tribunals in Geneva."

Here is my take. If people from usually opposing constituencies can concur on an important matter like these "pull-down" trade agreements without conceding any point for compromise, why not? Our critics would have had a point if I watered down my opposition to NAFTA and WTO to get Buchanan's agreement, but I wasn't going to do that. Nor was he.

Procedural agreements are far more possible to put together than substantive ones. This was a procedural opposition to a framework of enforceable rules that subordinated consumer, worker, and environmental standards to the supremacy of trade policy. These rules of sovereignty shifting did not remotely have the consent of the affected populations. Just the opposite was the case. They were to be implemented with great secrecy. Before the treaties were enacted under proposed fast-track legislation from the White House, Congress tied its own hands for a quick up or down vote with no amendments allowed.

There have been Left-Right procedural agreements going back generations. Many of the amendments in the Bill of Rights came to have this kind of broad consensus, starting with the First Amendment rights of freedom of speech, religion, petition, assembly, and press. We need to locate more procedural concurrence between Left and Right at less exalted heights in the many laws, agency policies, and obstructions to access to the courts that presently set up grossly unfair exclusions, leaving out the least powerful among us, who are often the vast majority.

A good illustration of convergence on procedural issues is LibCon support for restricting the state's power of eminent domain that authorizes corporations to forcibly take the property of others—homeowners, schools, and churches—demolish whatever is on it, and build a factory or enlarge a parking lot or a mall. This was what the city of Detroit empowered General Motors to do in the early eighties. GM asked for the use of the city's eminent domain powers to demolish hundreds of homes, numerous small businesses, schools, hospitals, and churches in order to clear out a stable, multiracial neighborhood of four hundred acres called Poletown. The purpose was to clear ground for a new GM plant that would have been built nearby, if not within the borders of Detroit. In the torrid struggle by the community to save itself from oblivion, recurrent nighttime arsons burned down one home after another. Visitors came to support their cause. They included progressive Democratic representative, now senator, Barbara Mikulski from Maryland and a leading libertarian, Fred Smith, of the Center for Competitive Enterprise. The Michigan Supreme Court, by a split vote, sided with GM and the mayor of Detroit. After the court decision, the neighborhood was leveled for the plant. A Cadillac plant was built with half of the jobs promised in return for over $300 million in local, state, and federal subsidies.[9]

Later, in 2005, when the Supreme Court upheld a state law of eminent domain (specifically to replace an entire neighborhood with the Pfizer corporation) by a 5–4 vote (liberals made up most of the five in favor, conservatives the four against) in the notorious *Kelo v. City of New London*, many state legislatures passed prohibitions on using eminent domain to replace private property with private property, winning these votes by lopsided margins of both Democrats and Republicans. There was clearly a Left-Right conjoining against this manifestation of statism garnished by crony capitalism—a combined force that could pass laws overwhelmingly.

This corporatization of eminent domain is part of a continuing struggle. Accordingly, it is fertile as a cause, if necessary through referenda, to bring customarily opposing blocs together, which can lead to other redirections of our society. These are referenda that corporations oppose but most of the people support, such as stopping taxpayer-funded commercial stadiums and ballparks or the California voters' initiative to raise the minimum wage to twelve dollars an hour, which is slated for November 2014 and advanced by conservative Ron Unz.

This latter is another area, among the many noted in this chapter, where Left-Right alliances are doable, though time and time again blocked by wily corporatists. In the next chapter, the major policies for Left-Right action outlines just how fertile the emerging political realignment can become.

4

Twenty-Five Proposed Redirections and Reforms Through Convergent Action

First the list:

1. Require that the Department of Defense (DOD) budget be audited annually, and disclose all government budgets. Secrecy destroys accountability.
2. Establish rigorous procedures to evaluate the claims of businesses looking for a government handout, which would end most corporate welfare and bailouts.
3. Promote efficiency in government contracting and government spending.
4. Adjust the minimum wage to inflation.
5. Introduce specific forms of taxation reform as well as push to regain uncollected taxes.
6. Break up the "Too Big to Fail" banks.
7. Expand contributions to charity, using them to increase jobs and drawing on available "dead money."
8. Allow taxpayers the standing to sue, especially immunized governments and corporations.

9. Further direct democracy—initiative, referendum, and recall, for starters.
10. Push community self-reliance.
11. Clear away the obstacles to a competitive electoral process.
12. Defend and extend civil liberties.
13. Enhance civic skills and experience for students.
14. End unconstitutional wars and enforce Article 1, section 8, of the Constitution, which includes the exclusive congressional authority to declare war.
15. Revise trade agreements to protect US sovereignty, and resume full congressional deliberations, ending fast track.
16. Protect children from commercialism and its physical and mental exploitation and harm.
17. End corporate personhood.
18. Control more of the commons that we already own.
19. Get tough on corporate crime, providing penalties and enforcement budgets.
20. Ramp up investor power by strengthening investor-protection laws and by creating a penny brigade to pay for an investor watchdog agency.
21. Oppose the patenting of life forms, including human genes.
22. End the ineffective war on drugs.
23. Push for environmentalism.
24. Reform health care.
25. Create convergent institutions.

It is important to think about *how to think about* convergence before we look over these proposed reforms. Otherwise, there will be too many wayward or excessive expectations, missed opportunities, and/or abrupt prejudgment about changes in one area after another. Herewith some guidelines:

First, for each agenda, divide the subject between procedural and substantive convergence. We can agree on a general policy or stance without having to also agree on the exact implications or use that would be made of a policy. For example, years ago LibCons agreed on the value of the federal and state Freedom of Information acts, which were directed to having a more open government. These laws can be used by anybody, regardless of who they are, and the requesters cannot be denied because of their motivation. So, let us imagine, one researcher may dig into the background of a Democratic governor's actions because the examiner is looking to expose corruption, while another may be looking into this same material because he or she is a partisan Republican desiring to expose any member of the other party. Each would have equal right to the records. Procedural stage 1 having been accomplished, with Freedom of Information acts passed, Lib-Cons will have to decide whether they agree on exactly what files or internal reports to obtain at any given time. That is the substantive stage.

Second, some of these initiatives can be advanced based on various positions or actions of the LCs over time that occur independently of one another, as long as they are solidly based on the principles and philosophies of liberalism and conservatism.

Third, whether or not there is a likelihood of the proposed reform being adopted or enacted in its entirety, the proper mindset is to aim high, but recognize that only a partial realization is possible at a given time. If one doesn't score the rare home run, then a single, double, triple, or run-saving catch or throw can be considered real progress.

Fourth, it may be worth the effort if we just commence a public discussion and debate on the topic. After all, everything starts with a conversation. Given the impoverishment of public and political dialogue these days, talking about something overcomes rooted self-censorship and shatters the taboos that have frozen freedom in the first place. If you visit our group's website, www.debating taboos.org, you'll see some actual debates shown on C-SPAN on usually taboo subjects as well as commentary about the necessity of confronting these typically unmentioned topics.

Fifth, in any given convergence, there will be uneven contributions by the LCs because one or the other has the most experience, best Rolodex, or more fire in the belly behind the desire to join together. This, naturally, is to be expected and welcomed. An illustration is Head Start, launched mostly by eager liberals but now backed by many conservatives because of its efficient effectiveness at early childhood education.

Sixth, even with concurrence on the goals, there will likely be difference over the means. Taxation reform is a prime illustration of this point. Conservatives and liberals are both in favor of it, but they have quite different ideas of how it should be done. Knowing this from the beginning may signal a temporary no-go or mean that each member of the alliance, having launched the demand for change together, can then proceed on their own to put forward their version of how it should be done.

Seventh, it is likely that the pioneers in any early convergence move will receive criticism from loyalists and invite career retaliation, ostracism, or some other expressions of disapproval. Pioneers must be prepared and able to stay true to their convictions.

Eighth, we can reasonably ask at what point on the continuum of LC collaboration can the effort be deemed to reach convergence? Is it when one L and one C converge? Or is there a critical mass needed to show that the convergence is really underway? The question is as hard to answer as this one: When does the Mississippi become a river, starting from its origins in drops of water in Minnesota that turn into rivulets, then brooks, streams, and tributaries? It is all in the flow, the direction, and the expanding replenishment. The various publics will notice when the takeoff occurs.

Ninth, when the LCs lock arms and get going, they will have to come together over what advocacy tools to use and what arenas to enter, considering what is available in a democratic society. Should they work through legislatures? The courts? Regulatory or procurement agencies? Should they work with entrepreneurs (commercial or nonprofit), those in the academic world, media, the retired, prominent persons, the enlightened super-rich, whistle-blowers, shareholders, grassroots campaigns? Ls and Cs often have different contacts, backgrounds, and tastes in connection with such levers of change, and how they are applied will have to be worked out in the same spirit of convergence.

Tenth, one noteworthy benefit of working on alliances is that the very experience with convergence stimulates the depth of our basic humanity and sense of justice. It is too easy to be cut off from others by narrow worldviews. Well-meaning, serious people are not immune to the infinite capacity of humans to self-deceive, to make their brain's capabilities prisoners of their cloistered, tunnel-vision minds. And when it involves the monistic merchant or commercial mind, especially that fostered by Big Business, we find this perspective responsible for some of the most astonishing absurdities. This is particularly visible in the way Big Business executives predicted calamities for their industries that are now seen as accepted, commonsense reforms and regulations. Businessmen publicly predicted that ending slavery and child labor, women achieving the vote, the creation of Social Security, and the introduction of auto and workplace safety would wreck their industries. (See http://cry wolfproject.org.)

Eleventh, these convergences require resources. First, money— the fuel for the solid development of effort. Convergers should devote real time and imagination to securing (if possible) a few enlightened super-rich, who may be in their seventies, eighties, and nineties, and composed of a different perspective toward life, the future, and posterity than that of their younger affluent friends. Our country is laden with leaden fortunes, basking in lassitudinous investments, some of whose possessors can be brought forth to advance our society in a way that would invigorate these generous donors with fresh significance. Let what follows be a preliminary menu of sorts for their tasting.

5

Getting to the Actions: Convergences Ahoy!

This is the point where we need to go over the reforms and directions list, looking at the key places where a convergence exists *in potentia* but needs to be coordinated for effective action. The first seven items on the list focus on economics in connection with such matters as the government's relationship to business contractors and the minimum wage.

1. Get the Department of Defense to audit its budget.

Even people accustomed to reading the Government Accountability Office (GAO) and investigative media reports about the mind-boggling waste, duplications, and corporate frauds in the Pentagon are astounded to learn that the Department of Defense cannot or will not make an annual audit of its sprawling $527 billion yearly budget, not counting the wars in Iraq and Afghanistan.[1] GAO auditors stationed at the Pentagon report *every year* to their principal—Congress—that the DOD's books are unauditable! Congress shrugs.

That is half of the entire discretionary budget of the US government. Unauditable budgets mean huge monies go astray. There is, for example, no audit trail for the $9 billion unaccounted for in the first months of the Iraq war.[2] One year the GAO caught the Air Force buying billions of dollars in spare parts because the service did not know that they already had these parts in some warehouses somewhere.[3]

Now there has been no polling on the public's attitude toward this colossal accounting gap, but I'll bet a demand for an auditable Pentagon budget would be supported by more than 90 percent of the population. Who in their right mind would run an operation like this? Well, someone who is big enough and can get away with it because the organization's funding pipeline, wrapped in patriotic flags, coming from Congress, and swarming with lobbyists for uncontested corporate contractors, is almost untouchable. Just about everybody knows this inside Congress, but they find it easier to self-censor and benefit from "feathering in their nest," as Howard Dean calls it, than to stand up against the policies that the Lockheed Martins, the Raytheons, the Boeings, and the General Dynamics corporations call a jobs program, especially as one or another of these firms and their subcontractors have operations in nearly every congressional district—420 out of 435, according to Dean.[4]

Still, setting the objective of having a Department of Defense budget capable of being audited is a perfect candidate for convergence. Anyone opposing this demand couldn't pass the laugh test. People from the Left-Right constituencies would flock to this cause if it gained traction, and if it became a reality, nobody would be more relieved than the GAO, plus the internal, beleaguered Pentagon auditors themselves and, maybe, the secretary of defense himself. Along these same lines, an analogous LR convergence-friendly demand would be that our legislators disclose all government budgets without exception.

2. Establish rigorous procedures to evaluate the claims of businesses looking for a government handout, which would end most corporate welfare and bailouts.

There are so many one-way corporate subsidies, handouts, give-aways, bailouts, and bloated contracting programs pouring out of Washington, DC, that there is no existing government compilation of them all. The reaction to the way Bush and Obama bailed out the Wall Street crooks and speculators was a flood of criticism from all directions, including from the Tea Partiers and the Occupy Wall Street participants. Those who voted for the string of bailouts in Congress were made to feel that the country would be backed onto an economic cliff if they didn't go along with the plans of Treasury Secretary Henry Paulson, who hailed from the lucrative helm of Goldman Sachs.

If we had a series of tests, proving such things as the validity and value of their claims, that corporate welfare seekers must pass, first in Congress and then in the agency or department that selects the takers, we would definitely cut out most of these multibillion-dollar freeloaders.

Presently, it is purely corporate lobbying and campaign cash that drives these gravy trains through Congress. Take the atomic energy industry, for example. Why should taxpayers bear the risk for tens of billions of dollars, the cost of financing and insuring atomic power plants? It is justified by the atomic power utilities saying the private financial markets won't loan and insure these white elephants without 100 percent federal government loan guarantees and the taxpayers' assumption of most of the liability in case of a disastrous meltdown. These reasons are not good enough. Such claims by the industry have never been carefully evaluated. Putting more rigorous, data-based criteria in the law as part of an annual approval process for any money disbursement to corporations would make Congress less vulnerable to sheer pressure politics from the corporatists.

Here's a perfect place for an LR coalition. Why wouldn't liberals and conservatives band together to stop these scandalous raids on the taxpayers? Many would, except those who are too occupied fighting battles over social issues and dialing for campaign dollars to take on corporate welfare reform that would lead to convergence.

3. Restore efficiency in government procurement.

At this point, government purchasing, a multitrillion dollar business—annually at the federal, state, and local levels—is over-ripe for huge savings and for obtaining better products and services. For too long, the full text of many procurement contracts has not been made public, too many are left without competitive bidding, and more often they are not even monitored during and after their completion. A bipartisan move passed Congress in 2004 requiring all agencies to put summaries of these contracts online. Similar bipartisan support exists for putting the entire texts online, as Indiana and Texas have done, but there has been no vigorous push to get this enacted as a result of the quiet opposition of the vendor industry, which does not like the sunlight. With entire texts online, more competitors are likely, taxpayer groups and the media can regularly monitor them for adherence or improvement in the terms on the next round, and scholars can delve deeply into this enormous, often sweetheart, contract state.

In 1988, the Center for Study of Responsive Law held a conference in Washington, DC, on government procurement to stimulate innovation, stressing how a fine-tuning of such contracts can create larger civilian markets. Earlier in this book, I noted the example of auto safety, in which air bags were introduced to cars via purchases by the government. One example in which procurements stimulated positive directions was the use of generic drugs by US Army purchase practices around World War II. And for years the navy, for economic reasons, was buying solar photovoltaics for remote locations. Solar energy advocates have used this fact in their activism.

Feelers for convergence have appeared in Congress (with Republican senator Tom Coburn teaming with Democrats), at the state level, in the literature, and in concrete examples, enough to suggest it is time to move to a larger stage. It is to be expected that objections will come from strict libertarians, who will say the true change would be to get the government out of most of these activities. That is another discussion, which will have to be gone through category by category. Here the convergent focus should be on the best and most honest use of the taxpayer dollar now.

4. Link the minimum wage with inflation.

A bottom-up convergence effort will be needed here to give the 70 percent plus support this measure has with the public a cutting edge in Congress. Over thirty million workers—hailing from varying political persuasions—are laboring at between the current $7.25 an hour (by far the lowest rate among the Western world's large countries) and the $10.50 per hour they would be getting if the 1968 minimum wage had been adjusted for inflation. This demand is going to get across-the-board support because a conservative worker at Walmart or McDonald's is not going to put any (perceived) antigovernment ideology ahead of his or her desire to put bread on the family table. And properly so.

Leading traditional conservative thinkers, with few exceptions, believed we needed to have a minimum, mandatory level of worker well-being. The exceptions do not believe in any minimum wage whatsoever, arguing, among other things, that it reduces the number of jobs that will be available. This is a stance that has been decisively rebutted by knowledgeable, published scholars, including Robert Pollin and other prominent economists.[5]

At least 70 percent of the population is behind an adjusted minimum wage, including Rick Santorum and, until 2012, Governor

Mitt Romney. With the outraged reactions that will be voiced when, for example, the full personal stories of what it is like for Mom and Dad to try to make it on $7.25 to $10.50 per hour when the bosses, like the CEOs of Walmart and Target, are making $11,000 or more per hour, reach the mass media, who has to worry about the claims of well-rewarded, armchair columnists?

5. Enact taxation reform, and gather uncollected taxes.

Taxation appears to be one of the more divisive issues among conservatives and liberals. Hardly a press opportunity goes by without no-tax, conservative (his description) House Speaker John Boehner decrying "all of the over-taxing, over-regulating, and over-spending that's going on in Washington."[6] Now switch to David Stockman, another Reagan conservative and former head of the White House's budget office in the early eighties. Retired after a long investment banking career, Stockman recently condemned the "simplistic and reckless idea that the way to stimulate the economy is to cut taxes anytime, anywhere, for any reason [which has] become embedded [in the GOP]. It has become a religion, it has become a catechism. It's become a mindless incantation."[7]

In fact, total income taxes paid by corporations or individuals as a percent of income and GDP in the United States is at the lowest level in decades.[8] That is a major reason why government deficits are expanding. Having less and less revenue to meet the spending levels of government, including its unpaid-for wars, results in trillion-dollar-plus deficits a year. Stockman says this plunge into red ink started with George W. Bush, who put forward massive increases in defense spending and large reductions in the revenue base while not making any effort at cutting spending of the corporate state.

What is Stockman's favorite tax? It would be one levied on financial transactions—in effect a sales tax on Wall Street speculation—one that could raise big money daily. Showing that one can never stereotype conservatives, even ones like Stockman, who would cut all kinds of federal social service and boondoggle military programs, he describes Wall Street in these words: "We have a massive casino that is doing nothing but churning transactions by the millisecond, robots trading with each other, as a result of the Federal Reserve juicing the system continuously with overnight money that's free. There's no productive value for Main Street or the real U.S. economy."[9]

A speculation tax on the hundreds of trillions of dollars annually spent chasing derivatives would not have to be more than one-half of 1 percent to raise $300 billion a year. The European Commission proposed such a tax as well. Eleven European countries already have some lesser form of transaction tax.[10]

Such a tax is an easy sell to shoppers, who have to pay a 6 to 8 percent (or more) retail sales tax in stores when they buy the necessities of life. LR shoppers is where the convergence can start, but to get off the ground it would need some high-profile political leadership and media reporting and commentary. I've often joked that we won't get such a financial transaction tax, one championed, by the way, by many an organized nurses' rally, unless leading financial columnists for the *New York Times*, Floyd Norris and Gretchen Morgenson, get on the issue.

But I think it is more promising to start a dialogue outside the box of this LR wrangling over the tax rates for income, capital gains, and dividends (I believe they should all be taxed at the same rate). Thinking outside the box, we might consider proposing that before taxes on work or labor, there should be taxation of what society likes the least or dislikes the most, so as to diminish these activities. For example, tax carbon pollution, a policy favored by Exxon/Mobil, several leading Republicans, liberal and conservative economists, and many environmentalists. And tax financial speculation; hike gambling taxes and taxes on addictive products like tobacco, alcohol, and certain addictive drugs; raise the penalties on corporate crime along with other harmful activity; and do all that before going for worker incomes.

Conservative Nobel laureate in economics Gary S. Becker, former secretary of the treasury George P. Shultz, and former chief economic adviser to President George W. Bush, N. Gregory Mankiw, are leading proponents of a carbon tax or a gasoline tax to pay for the damage (called "externalities" by economists) of motor vehicle traffic. Canadian reformers have a saying for this: "Tax what we burn, not what we earn." I would add: "Tax first what we bet, not what we net." When I discuss these ideas before mixed audiences, I find much convergent interest in those kinds of tax priorities, although some want the carbon tax to be revenue-neutral. But we won't really know if these out-of-the-box proposals have traction unless some politicians and a few corporate leaders like Warren Buffett lead the way in giving the ideas visibility and credibility and then help the people mobilize.

As to the chronic matter of owed but uncollected taxes, where the miscreants are flouting the law, signing on should be an easy decision for conservatives. Such flouting is unfair to those who pay taxes and have to pay more or receive fewer services. It amounts, says the IRS, to more than $300 billion a year in tax evasion! This is not tax avoidance, the type practiced by corporate interests that legally use tax havens and have many other arcane ways they have pushed through Congress to escape taxes; it is a violation of the law. Amazingly, many conservatives and libertarians I have spoken with over time view this as a sport, as if cheating is making up for the too many taxes people have to pay. Because of this attitude, this issue may have to be shelved for a more auspicious time of convergent resolution.

6. Break up the "too big to fail" banks.

Conservative columnist George Will put the judgment pithily: a financial institution that is "too big to fail is too big to exist."[11]

Richard W. Fisher, the president of the Federal Reserve Bank of Dallas, delivered a detailed address in January 2013 on just how to disaggregate these banks in a top-to-bottom restructuring, so that no one giant bank can imperil the financial system and require another gigantic taxpayer bailout. Out of more than 5,600 US commercial banks, Fisher says, "half of the entire banking industry's assets are in the hands of five institutions"—JP Morgan Chase, Bank of America, Citigroup, Wells Fargo, and US Bancorp. "This incurs the wrath of ordinary citizens," Fisher adds, "and smaller entities that resent this 'favorable treatment.' . . . [Through encouraging these big banks] we plant the seeds of social unrest." Perversely, the big bank bailouts under Bush and Obama required immediate mergers and acquisitions that more than doubled this concentration of banking assets and deposits.

Too-big-to-fail (TBTF) guarantees profits because it socializes losses. Mr. Will expresses why this subject is an immediate subject for ideological and legislative convergence: "TBTF is a double moral disaster. It creates moral hazard by encouraging risky behavior and it delegitimizes capitalism by validating public cynicism about its risk-reward ratios."[12] Most members of Congress, liberal and conservative, agree that TBTF must end, but as Senator Richard Durbin (D-IL) said, "The banks . . . frankly, own the place."[13]

Perhaps what he should have said was that "the banks bought this place." If the votes are there, with the smaller banks, consumers, and taxpayers at their back, members of Congress can un-buy themselves, at least for the limited purpose of prohibiting TBTF and letting market discipline prevail to that extent.

7. Expand and redirect contributions to charity.

How about a job creation convergence, which could be based on encouraging large charitable contributions from the rich and super-rich to local educational and charitable organizations needing more staff? This involves a national vision made possible by local networking and outreach to persuade donors that if they like what private charities are doing for children, needy people, the arts, sports, the environment, literacy, historic preservation, and more, then contributing enough to expand the staff budget means the charities can hire more people, which spells the magic word these days—JOBS!

The arithmetic is impressive. There are trillions of dollars held by upper-income Americans in what might be called "inert" investments, many in money market funds, savings banks, and treasuries, bringing in a fraction of 1 percent in interest. Almost all the people holding these monies are nowhere near their annual charitable deduction limit of 50 percent of adjusted gross income. Lamentably, many also give very little to charitable associations. Most could save more in taxes from their charitable contributions than by keeping the money in near zero-interest savings.

For each billion dollars in aggregate extra charitable donations per year to existing or new certified charitable associations to *expand staff*, 30,000 people could be hired at a salary around $30,000 a year. Ten billion additional dollars would produce 300,000 jobs all across the country, enlarging the good works of these organizations, which, in turn, produce their own human and economic savings. Think of the collateral benefits of safety programs; food banks; elder care; historic renovations sprucing up communities; sports programs for youngsters; more human assistance between the generations; support groups for the disabled and infirm; arts, crafts, and music activities; and quicker, adequate help for families or neighborhoods beset by the aftermaths of natural calamities, street crimes, domestic violence, and accidents.

As the *Chronicle of Philanthropy* reports, the unmet needs and opportunities are endless, and the willing talent pool only grows in a recession with high unemployment.[14]

One sterling way to launch the initiative, which, of course, is wonderfully nonpartisan, is for the president to speak before a large convocation of charitable groups (many of whom have had to lay off staff due to reduced budgets) and make the point that larger capabilities with expanded staffs, funded by whatever the target dollar figure is, will benefit millions of Americans and create jobs. Often presidents from either party visit factories as a way to highlight job creation, lugging their bully pulpits with them. And these presidents always give lip service to the good works of charities. So this should not be a difficult transition, matching these two themes, once the imaginative dynamic is introduced to the White House by a visiting Grand Convergence delegation.

The next set of six proposals deals with increasing democracy.

8. *Loosen the current legal restrictions on standing to sue.*

People who are not lawyers may not realize that an individual's right to bring a lawsuit against certain parties for specific outrages is severely restricted in the US courts. A person can only bring suit if the court believes the individual has the proper "standing to sue," traditionally defined as possessing "a distinct and palpable, redressable injury." The standing-to-sue doctrine was originally conceived centuries ago in England to discourage litigators with no discrete, tangible stake in the case from filing suit, then losing interest and dropping out.

This issue has never been raised in our major party political campaigns. But if we view the courts as the last bastion of freedom from arbitrary, abusive power, and for the fundamental liberties of the people, then the door-closer that judges have when they say a person who wants to bring suit has no standing to sue comprises a critical abdication by our third branch of government. Access to the courts and the right of trial by jury were major bones of contention for the patriots who overthrew King George III. You may remember that second on their celebrated list of grievances, drawn up in 1774, coming right after "no taxation without representation," was the charge that the king was excluding them from being judged by a jury of their peers—a definitive right they were later to put in the Seventh Amendment to our Constitution.

Today, libertarians often speak of their opposition to regulation by saying that access to the courts is the way to deal with harms inflicted by others. Jeno F. Paulucci, the late, immensely successful businessman who called himself an independent-minded conservative Republican, relished using the courts to obtain justice, including for those poor people whom he freed from their wrongful imprisonment. When I notified him about my quest to start the first law museum in America, he enthusiastically sent me a quotation from lawyer and president John Adams, clearly a conservative hero, in which the statesman eloquently approved of filing lawsuits to "procure redress to wrongs, the advancement of right, to assert and maintain liberty and virtue, [and] to discourage and abolish tyranny and vice."[15]

Now consider what the continual opposition by the government and the courts to the standing-to-sue right as a way to block access to courts for Americans, rich and poor, who cannot, in John Adam's words, "discountenance the haughty and lawless."[16] Time and again, ordinary taxpayers, no matter how many come together as plaintiffs, cannot get through the courtroom door to challenge the largest, most documented wasteful or violative programs involving, say, military or software contractors or mining on public lands. Nor can they legally protest against financial frauds, state subsidies to lure companies from other states, or ongoing taxpayer theft in the form of government contract corruption tied to corporate criminals, to select the obvious examples. The federal courts regularly say that the citizen plaintiffs have no standing to sue. Moreover, take this example: Arizona taxpayers wanted to challenge the state's tuition tax credit, which was giving money to private, religious schools, on grounds of separation of church and state (the Establishment Clause of the Constitution). The Supreme Court of the United States ruled that they lacked standing to sue.[17]

What would happen if citizens, including members of Congress, sued to stop a war of choice that Congress had neither declared nor authorized nor appropriated monies? The courts would dismiss the case either for lack of standing or on the grounds that it is a "political question" to be resolved by the other two branches of government. The judges are not bothered by the fact that the two branches do not want to resolve it precisely for political reasons. Or how about a *mandamus* action (in which the court stops an institution from doing or not doing specific actions) in the egregious cases in which the executive department or agency is flouting a law by neither enforcing it nor meeting reporting deadlines to Congress. Such cases are brought frequently and are as frequently met by judges who stop them by invoking no standing to sue. Who might indeed have standing to sue in such cases? One person only—the attorney general of the United States—an unlikely plaintiff, especially as he owes his position to the president and is supposed to defend agencies, not prosecute them.

If conservatives and liberals are on the record historically and repeatedly as demanding governmental accountability, then having Congress provide flexible criteria to expand the standing-to-sue doctrine should be a prime candidate for convergence. Advocates can point to many procedurally dismissed cases, which have been brought by party faithfuls from both sides, as one warrant to justify their joining together.

9. Expand direct democracy.

When a former used car salesman, Ed Koupal, and his wife, Joyce, began their rise from utter powerlessness to being key champions of citizens' power through the establishment of a statewide volunteer network in California, which would work to qualify ballot initiatives by getting large numbers of voters' signatures on petitions, they were not relying on one specific group of ideologues to help them. They tapped into the widest possible group of citizens of different persuasions. It was from this diverse pool of voters that they drew their signatures, putting up tables in various high-density locations, such as shopping centers or convention and civic centers. Before cancer struck and ended their populist ascent, leading politicians, including governors, would call to ask their advice or try to curry favor from their volunteer network, a rising civic juggernaut of direct democracy, with two major statewide initiative wins to its credit.

About twenty-four states—mostly west of the Mississippi—have this citizen right of direct democracy through ballot initiatives. Many more municipalities, especially in New England, have this form of people power, dating back to the eighteenth century. But most states and localities do not allow such practices or, if they do, they are very hard for citizens to use without going through onerous hoops, including approval by state legislatures.

There are liberal and conservative groups that do not like this type of people's initiative or referendum (in which decision on an issue is put to the people) or recall (in which an elected lawmaker can be put out of office by a citizen vote). Liberals who are against such practices include most labor unions, which fear corporate funded restrictions. Conservatives who don't back them include right-wingers who dread "the rabble" and cite James Madison's preference for only "representative government."

But the polls suggest direct democracy is a necessity. So many voters sit out elections of candidates, thinking they have little say in who is nominated. If we afforded them the opportunity to be part of the process via the procedures of direct democracy, they would no longer have any excuse to opt out. Another benefit of direct democracy is the way it can be a watchdog over the legislatures, ready to move the body politic forward when, as is often the case, the lawmakers freeze because of interest group lobbying and money.

Let me give you an example of the effectiveness of direct democracy. In 1988, together with Harvey Rosenfield and others, I

led a campaign in California to enact, via a ballot initiative, a law
that required the auto insurance companies to open their books.
Whenever they want a rate increase, they now have to prove their
case by showing their need before approval or rejection by the state
insurance commissioner. The insurers spent a record $80 million
against our $2 million, yet we defeated them and enacted Proposi-
tion 103. More than $102 billion dollars have been saved by Cal-
ifornia consumers so far. The companies that threatened to leave
the state are now making more money than ever, but under a more
rigorous underwriting system.[18]

There is a strong convergence potential that could be marshaled
to spread the initiative, referendum, and recall to every state and
municipality. Moreover, there is a constitutional case to be made,
as some law professors and former senator Mike Gravel argue, for
our country to have a binding national referendum right for the
consideration of significant issues, under careful procedures and
conditions. This could be easily justified by the old Roman adage
"Whatever touches all should be decided by all."

10. Organize encouragement and patronage of community-rooted businesses.

Such businesses would include credit unions, community banks,
farmer-to-consumer markets, local renewable energy producers,
community health clinics, and assorted consumer-owned cooperatives. This couldn't be more convergent—pleasing to both liberals
and conservatives. It is private enterprise, born of and staying in
the community, mostly small business, whose existence enhances
community self-reliance, returning our society to traditional ways
and avoiding dependency on absentee control by domestic or
foreign multinational corporations, such as big banks, big energy
companies, big hospitals, and big food-processing conglomerates.
Yes! magazine chronicles specific community-rooted enterprises

often enabled by modern technologies and many other expanding community economies in almost every issue. *Yes!* also delves into the fusion of consumer and producer, such as we see in food gardens, arts and crafts, time/dollar collaborations, neighborhood day care centers, community bookstores, and other facilities that are knitters of community life in America.

What's not to like? Community self-reliance strengthens families, reduces long commutes that separate families from children, insulates local assets and savings from the speculative tumult, and avoids the excessive interdependence that can generate financial contagion, which is often a negative result of corporate globalization (as seen, for example, in small Greece shaking the stock markets of Europe and the United States). It further fortifies the connectedness of kin, neighborhood, and community that make for good, nurturing life. Where's the downside? Convergence and our consumer dollars, here we come!

11. Clear away the obstacles to a competitive electoral process.

Let's begin by looking at how a two-party monopoly controls the US political system and what it costs. Start with the reality that no Western democracy presents the kinds of barriers to voting generally and to third parties or independent candidates running for elective office as do the various states of the United States. Not surprisingly, no other Western country is so completely dominated by two major parties, which predictably, given where the money and power comes from for their campaigns, are both converging on adherence to corporatism.

Candidate rights are inextricably related to voting rights. Very limited candidate choices under a two-party junta that gerrymanders electoral districts, so that they will be subject to domination by one or the other major party, depreciates voter rights. A wider range of candidates would give voters more voices and choices.

The existing system is perverse. Most voters are "represented" by one party's dominated district's incumbent. Currently 80 percent of the members of the House of Representatives are such incumbents.[19] Both major parties erect harsh and costly barriers to hinder small challengers from getting on the ballot. Petitioners, garnering names to help get an independent or third party candidate on the ballot, are harassed on the streets, and fake names are signed for sabotage. Baseless lawsuits are filed by the major parties' large law firms to drain away the resources and time of small candidates, and when the cases come to court, the independent often finds that a partisan judge, known for political loyalty, is on the bench. I experienced all this and more in my presidential campaigns. My campaign manager, Theresa Amato, meticulously documented many of the outrages in her book *Grand Illusion: The Myth of Voter Choice in a Two-Party Tyranny.*[20]

These myriad barriers may be condemned as a violation of laws protecting civil rights and civil liberties, and they certainly derail proposed reforms and policy redirections that an independent candidate may offer to the voters. That critique is probably the liberal/progressive take or is that of liberals who are not silenced by going along with the least-worst mindset.

The parallel libertarian, free market approach is taken by economics professor James T. Bennett of George Mason University. He sees a two-party duopoly, protected and subsidized by the government it controls, as a way to block any external competition and make sure that no third party or independent candidate would even have a chance to compete and grow in strength over the span of successive elections. Bennett wants to abolish the subsidies to the major parties and get rid of the ballot-access barriers to entry and other trip-points. He approves the words of progressive professor Theodore J. Lowi: "It is time to deregulate American politics, letting it take whatever form it will."[21] Bennett wants to close down the two-party controlled Federal Election Commission. He doesn't even like the idea of organized parties, reminding us of many of the founding fathers' deep distaste for parties or character-twisting "factions," as they called them, before they finally resigned themselves to their formation. "Like Madison," writes Bennett in his recent book *Stifling Political Competition: How Government Has Rigged the System to Benefit Demopublicans and Exclude Third Parties*, "John Adams was resigned to the existence of parties, but he stressed they must not be permitted to plunder the treasury."[22]

There is convergence here between the likes of Amato and Bennett, but it only goes so far, because of disagreements over whether the state would referee and level the playing field in a reformed system. Amato thinks this is possible. Bennett believes the state will always be manipulated to serve the two-party duopoly—now via subsidies, exclusive debates, and the funding of the two major party conventions by taxpayers. Each side's view of the flaws in the current arrangement are good starts, but once again liberals and conservatives have to drop their corporatist and two-party allegiances and look straight at the reforms that are needed to give more choices for the voters in a competitive democracy. The convergent groups Citizens in Charge and Free and Equal are already at work on this objective. Working toward this goal may be much easier to commence at the community level, where the sense of fairness is greater than among those in the national professional party circles and their acolytes.

12. Defend and extend civil liberties.

This cause received a shot of adrenaline in 2002, when ex-FBI agent and Republican congressman Bob Barr joined with the American Civil Liberties Union (ACLU) to protest the Bush administration's abuses through the PATRIOT Act, which included unlawful surveillance and invasions of citizen privacy. In truth, this kind of Left-Right alliance has been long overdue, and thanks can be given to the violations perpetuated by Bush and Cheney and continued under Obama that more LibCon alliances are being forged.

Convergence around civil liberties can be seen in the filing of lawsuits regarding arrests and jailing without charges, and massive unlawful surveillance, and in the joint opposition to heavy-handed airport passenger searches that are conducted with ineffective, risky screening machines, even while cargo still is not fully checked twelve years after 9/11. Numerous conferences on civil liberties are now routinely attended by the most unlikely of customary adversaries.

Yet it must be said that for the better part of a century, the fight for civil liberties was identified with the liberal Left. Right-wingers have strived to make the ACLU name into a dirty word, suggesting that pushing for civil liberties indicates a mark of softness on everything from crime to communism. Then the security leviathan began to encompass the totality of Americans. The mass surveillance program of the Defense Advanced Research Projects Agency (DARPA), conducted through the Information Awareness Office, brought a bipartisan denunciation from Congress before it was technically terminated and defunded in 2003. In reality, it was merely dispersed to other intelligence agencies, such as the CIA and the National Security Agency (NSA), which proved smarter in their avoidance of naming what they were expansively doing, all with Obama's approval. The explosive disclosures of Edward Snowden and other whistle-blowers in 2013 revealed the program to be very expansive here and over our foreign allies.

There really is no easy way, under either party, to stop a continuation of government surveillance of citizens, using penetrating technologies and equipped with the rationale of a permanent war against terror. On September 28, 2011, the Left-Right Alliance Against Government Reading Your Email Without a Warrant campaign was launched. The aligned groups included the Center for Democracy and Technology (L), the Americans for Tax Reform (R), the Bill of Rights Defense Committee (L), the Competitive Enterprise Institute (R), the ACLU (L), the Electronic Frontier Foundation (L/R), and Tech Freedom (R). About the same time, Apple went public, speaking out against government searches of electronic devices without a warrant. The firm joined the organization Digital Due Process, made up of Amazon, AT&T, Google, HP, and Microsoft, which asserts that the members "are working to improve privacy for smartphone, tablet and computer users."[23]

These companies often find the FBI, along with other intelligence and enforcement agencies, coming to them with requisitioning security letters and other demands for private information about their customers. These firms are in a conflict between their customers and the government, for they may be forced to give up personal computer files and invade their customers' privacy. This issue has brought people of constitutional sensitivities together, even while they disagree with each other on many political matters.

Call it a procedural or piecemeal convergence. Freedom and privacy will take whatever they can get these days. On this issue, the Right needs to catch up for a real convergence to get moving. The Left puts far more money and staff into these struggles, and now the Right should be matching the progressives.

13. Expand the civic skills and experience of students from elementary to secondary schools.

This redirection seems self-evidently necessary. If there is no convergence over this important, generic educational advancement, the reason has to be that personal animosities on other matters are poisoning local relations between the two political persuasions. In that case, someone on either or both sides should say, "Get over it." The essence of wisdom starts with transcending lesser conflicts in favor of the greater common good. Giving our children civic skills is so necessary for the future of a democratic society and accountability of government, corporations, and other institutions of power that it invites the Latin phrase *res ipsa loquitur* (the thing speaks for itself). And it's not just party partisans that are blocking progress. School boards are so riven with bitter quarrels or so willing to turn themselves into compliant supplicants trying to raise funds for the educational fad of the year, such as putting a computer in front of every ten-year-old, that they fail to appreciate the importance of civic education and civic experience.

A coming together in the struggle against civic abdication, student apathy, virtual reality, gadgetry, ignorance of history and public affairs, and detachment from community can become a unifying force, which moves our schools beyond personalities, fads, and the wrongheaded emphasis on high-frequency standardized testing. This effort, along with restoring physical education classes to improve children's health, is a battle that needs to be fully joined.

Now let me mention a couple of convergence points that deal with our nation's relations to foreign governments and globalized companies.

14. End unconstitutional wars and unchecked militarism.

Inspired by the military actions of the Clinton administration, the Obama and Bush teams made a seamless transition into a militarized foreign policy, extending even further the illegal reach of wars of choice, invasions, incursions, and drone attacks, carried out irrespective of national sovereignties. From libertarians to progressives, from conservatives to liberals (from the *American Conservative* to the *Nation*), one hears about the "American Empire" in one headline after another that speaks about some of the downsides of our military ventures, fueled by a relentless, bloody hubris, which has no compunction about breaking constitutional restraints, federal statutes, budgets, international treaties, and the system of checks and balances. All these lead an overweening executive, a rubber-stamp Congress, and a judiciary abjuring any jurisdiction. In fact, in 2013 a debate over the military and domestic use of drones broke out, sparked by Senator Rand Paul's twelve-hour filibuster, which brought together mainstream conservative and liberal think tanks, Republican and Democratic lawmakers, and citizen activists of both Right and Left.

Many former high military, diplomatic, and national security officials, who have served under both parties, spoke out forcefully against the invasion of Iraq in March 2003. These included retired Marine general Anthony Zinni, retired general and head of the National Security Agency Howard Odom, and even the first President Bush's top international advisers, Brent Scowcroft and James Baker. I counted about three hundred retirees in these three categories (military, diplomatic, and national security) who spoke out before the invasion once or more, individually. But there was no infrastructure to aggregate them into a persistent force and repeatedly publicize their detailed critiques in the crucial nine-month run-up to the invasion. Add to these antiwar voices the dozens of congressional Democrats, liberal and progressive magazines, and commentators who were challenging the same falsehoods, distortions, and cover-ups by the White House that those prominent retirees were condemning. What an opportunity there was for an organized convergence of those two groups that would have stopped this long, costly war, so destructive of Iraq, its people, our soldiers, our laws, our stressed budgets, and our country's security and diplomatic status in the world!

The same belligerent process can be unleashed again and again, as indeed it has been in smaller and larger ways in Afghanistan, Pakistan, Libya, Yemen, Somalia, and other nations. Anticipatory convergence is essential to prevent more of these provocations and aggressions that are banking future revenge against America by angry people related to the many dead civilians, as well as bankrupting our country in so many ways.

George Soros, worth an estimated $23 billion, was a strong open and public opponent of the Iraq war. And had he provided, say, $200 million worth of strategic resources to put behind the patriotic retired leaders, helping them mobilize people to send a decisive message to Congress, it would have exposed and stopped the prevarication-strewn drive to war on Iraq. The American people would have learned of the army's opposition to the war, which went all the way up to four-star generals, who were muzzled. Even now, during the neocon and Israeli government drumbeats to attack Iran, it would still be timely for him to provide the media infrastructure and organizational resources so as to bring together these former officials—liberals and conservatives—in a permanent, high-level watchdog network, poised to prevent such reckless, blowback wars. The path was being trail-blazed in 2012 by a small, new group: the National Commission on Intelligence and Foreign Wars. Its members, including retired military, reflect a Left-Right concurrence focusing on Congress. In July 2013, what had been simmering erupted with a Left-Right rebellion against the Republican and Democratic leaders in the House of Representatives to almost win a ban on the NSA's blanket snooping on the domestic telephone and email communications of the American people. The vote was 217–205.[24]

15. Revise NAFTA, WTO, and similar trade agreements in favor of greater justice.

This touches the desires of both liberals and conservatives. These pacts are not your free trade treaties of modern history that involved smaller tariffs or ending quotas. As we've seen, they are international systems of autocratic governments, with severe penalties for infringement, which go far beyond reducing the aforementioned trade barriers. They subordinate consumer, worker, and environmental protections to the imperatives of global trade by labeling any country with high safeguards in these sectors as erecting "nontariff trade barriers," which are illegal and prosecutable by the bureaucrats in Geneva on request by a member nation having lesser safeguards. That's why I call these trade treaties "pull-down agreements." Conflicts are resolved by circumventing member countries' agencies, courts, and legislatures in favor of literally secret courts, which operate without independent appellate review, behind closed doors in Switzerland, where neither the media nor anyone else (except direct advocates from the contending countries) can witness what's going on.

Test what people think of this loss of sovereignty, this overriding of our democratic practices, this undermining of our workers' jobs and well-being, this unfair competition from countries brutalized by their rulers (e.g., by using child labor, which under the WTO can be exploited to manufacture goods sold abroad, whose imports cannot be prohibited by other signatory nations, including the United States). Talk to conservatives and liberals about our country being defenseless, unable to block countries with lower safety standards that want to export food and medicines here. Thousands of Americans have died or gotten sick or defrauded just by using contaminated products from China, which has not allowed full FDA inspections. Other provisions in these agreements, always negotiated in secret, except for "consultations" with the corporate lobbies, would sear the sensibilities of just about all Americans of whatever persuasion, who experience the consequences in their daily lives. Yet the corporatists in both parties are pushing for even more autocratic agreements, such as the all-secret TransPacific partnership being negotiated with Asian nations. Lori Wallach, director of Global Trade Watch, describes this draft treaty by the United States as "enforceable corporate global governance . . . that could rip up our basic needs and rights."[25]

Language in every one of these ratified treaties allows signatory nations to give six months' notice of withdrawal. An economy the size of the United States signaling its intention to give six months' notice would bring the others rushing quickly to the negotiating table for revision. Global Trade Watch, a durable coalition of Left-Right allies from civic, labor, and corporate groups that has long been in opposition to these agreements, has the details of how these negotiations should be conducted to be fair to Americans and other peoples in the world. (See Global Trade Watch at http://www.citizen.org/trade/.)

This issue is ready-made for convergence and "shovel-ready" for donations sufficient to do the job.

The next five redirections concern corporate abuses.

16. *Guard our children from commercialism.*

About fifteen years ago, as described earlier, I spoke to an audience of evangelical Christians in Washington, DC. They were not of my political persuasion, nor were they glowing with expectant approbation as I approached the lectern. My topic was the brazen commercialism in direct contradiction of religious values and parental authority—namely, the daily, hourly, pervasive commercialization of childhood in America. Through direct marketing to children as young as three or four years old, advertisers bypass parents and sell junk food and drink—health-harming products—broadcast violent programming, and, at a later age, promote addictive products, such as tobacco, alcohol, and medications. Whole generations of youngsters are being harmed physically and mentally. I observed that it didn't matter what your politics are, you have to agree that this is wrong and had to be opposed. They gave me an enthusiastic reception. Parents understand but are often too discouraged to fight against commercialism; many feel overwhelmed by relentless, seductive marketing aimed directly at their children and their peer groups.

Clearly, how to defend our children from these inroads could be a unifying mission. There is already some existing converging activity from Foundations Family Counseling, Commercial Alert, Focus on the Family, and Parenting.com that needs much higher visibility and resources, as well as more aggressive convergence.

17. Get rid of corporate personhood.

I already cited an article by former high-ranking Republican conservative and Wyoming senator Alan Simpson calling for campaign finance reform and criticizing the Supreme Court's *Citizens United* decision, which allowed the opening of unlimited spigots for the contribution of corporate cash to political campaigns. He especially excoriated the court's Republican majority for "asserting a remarkable right of corporate personhood that I have yet to find in the Constitution."

The personhood idea originated with the scribe who reported the 1886 Supreme Court decision in the *Santa Clara County v. Southern Pacific Railroad Company* case and put in the head notes on the decision something the justices expressly *did not decide*. He erroneously or maliciously wrote—he was a former railroad employee— that the railroad in the case is considered a "person" for purposes of the Fourteenth Amendment. After that, it was off to the races, with one Supreme Court case after another using that misconstruction to assert the existence of other "person" rights for that artificial entity, chartered by the state, called a "corporation." However, the conservatives' conservative jurist of our generation, Chief Justice William Rehnquist, was not fully persuaded of the validity of these claims. Rehnquist's dissent from Associate Justice Lewis Powell's majority opinion in the Pacific Gas and Electric case (1986) still stands as a bright red line drawn to block the granting of full First Amendment powers for corporations that broke the emerging consumer checkoff movement. The California state regulators had allowed a consumer advocacy organization to place inserts in utility billing envelopes, at no cost to the utility, inviting residential ratepayers to join a dues-paying consumer advocacy group on utility issues—economic or environmental. The majority Supreme Court opinion saw this as violating the utility's First Amendment rights to remain silent and not have to rebut declarations made in the insert.

In stark contrast to his Republican colleague on the court, Lewis Powell, an arch-corporatist advocate of businesses' constitutional rights, the dissenting Justice Rehnquist believed giving corporations free speech rights that assume a conscience is to "confuse metaphor with reality," adding that "the 14th Amendment does not require a state to endow a business corporation with the power of political speech."

As Jeffrey D. Clements writes in his fine book *Corporations Are Not People*, Rehnquist "grounded his dissents in the fundamental proposition that our Bill of Rights sets out the rights of *human beings* and that corporations are not people. For years, Rehnquist maintained this principled conservative argument, warning over and over again that such corporate rights have no place in our republican form of government."[26] Before *Citizens United* overturned previous legal precedents, Rehnquist's views had won over a majority of his fellow justices. This position appeared especially in the *Austin v. Michigan Chamber of Commerce* case, in which the court upheld a Michigan law regulating corporate spending in elections.

Chief Justice William Rehnquist remains, after his passing in 2005, a far more authoritative judicial and philosophical figure in conservative circles than does Powell, a corporate lawyer (for the tobacco companies and other giant companies) later turned corporatist jurist.

Although getting rid of the legal validity of corporate personhood has been a prime object for reform in liberal circles, thanks in no small part to the prodigious writing, lecturing, and organizing efforts of the late Richard Grossman, it is only beginning to take hold in conservative circles, spurred toward this position by their libertarian allies. The Transpartisan Alliance, led by libertarian

Michael Ostrolenk, is networking with those of all possible political persuasions to, in Clements's words, "restrain the government-created and subsidized transnational corporations that wield such power over American lives and communities."[27]

The coming battle over corporate personhood, further provoked by the recent Supreme Court decision in *Citizens United* and its subsequent anti–states' rights decision in *American Tradition Partnership, Inc. v. Steve Bullock, Attorney General of Montana*, which overruled a venerable Montana law prohibiting corporate money in elections, is no internal arcane dispute among lawyers. Without the privileges and immunities of corporate personhood, companies can be subordinated to the priorities and supremacy of "we the people," that is, the sovereignty of the people so clearly enunciated in the words of the Constitution.

The radical judicial legislation that has been promoting the idea of corporate personhood since 1886 flies in the face of the bare fact that there is absolutely no mention of the word "corporation," "company," or "artificial entity" in the text of the Constitution as amended. Overturning the decisions based on this illegitimate idea of corporate personhood would mean that people, if they chose, could legislatively and judicially redress much of the imbalance of power between them and corporations. If corporations cannot claim the same constitutional rights as natural persons, the people will be able to better control, for instance, harmful and violent commercial marketing to children as well as put an end to the ways companies are taxed, prosecuted, subsidized, coddled, and allowed to prevent people from banding together. This is what I believe Russell Kirk meant when he listed "prudent restraints upon power"[28] as a conservative principle and what historical liberalism meant by restraining the state from so empowering large corporations. The way these points, from opposite ends of the political spectrum, echo each other indicates that on this issue there is a convergence waiting to mature.

18. Control more of the public commons we already own.

This is a basic principle of capitalism, which has been restricted at times for good reasons, as when it is applied by a government's eminent domain to take lands needed for public highways, bridges, and other traditional public works. But we've already seen how eminent domain has been perverted to take private property for corporate, not government, uses.

For generations corporations have also been overthrowing traditional notions of property rights in cases in which the property is either held in trust for many or collectively owned by all. I am referring, of course, to *the commons*—that great reservoir of public wealth known as the public lands, the public airwaves, public works, public investments, and recently the widening commons of the Internet/cyberspace and the oceans. Through astonishing giveaways, as has happened with the people's hard-rock minerals (gold, silver, etc.) on federal lands, or through bargain-basement leases, giving companies the right to extract other valuable natural resources, corporations get control and profitably use what we own. Also, bear in mind that we are the landlords of the public airwaves; the broadcasters are the tenants. Yet, they pay no rent, get free usage twenty-four hours a day, and unilaterally decide who gets on and who is excluded. Not fair! Major modern industries were created or hugely nurtured by taxpayer-paid research and development monies. These include the aerospace, biotech, nanotech, computer and Internet, pharmaceutical, medical device, containerization, and agribusiness industries.

Controlling what we own would involve charging market prices, reserving some of the owned assets for direct public use (such as time slots for an audience-controlled TV and radio network), and using public investments or purchasing as leverage to obtain safer products, workplaces, and environments or to help further national missions benefiting all.

This is a thorny topic, which will split the conservative/libertarian cohort deeply along a whole range of differences. Some will say the government should sell off the public lands and airwaves, get out of industry developing, and just corporatize public works such as highways. Others would argue that government should run these taxpayer assets "as a business," as long as they hold them in trust for the public.

On the liberal/progressive side, some would say that the government should take greater control, having, for example, an equivalent to the British Broadcasting Corporation and Canadian Broadcasting Corporation on radio and television, or having a trust fund drawn from royalties earned from mining public lands, which would dispense regular checks to each American, the way the oil trust fund does in Alaska for every Alaskan. David Bollier and his colleagues in the spreading commons movement (http://onthecommons.org) are thinking through many proposals for more conserving, efficient, and equitable management of these public resources. Notably, the largest permanent marine reserve, off the coast of Hawaii, was created at the initiative of President George W. Bush.

Although we've seen that the two sides do not see eye to eye on this topic, there are still opportunities here, there, and everywhere to reach convergence on particular issues, while avoiding a massive, omnibus ideological showdown. Both Lou Dobbs and Bill O'Reilly of Fox News recognized that the people own the oil and gas discovered on public lands, and Dobbs proposed a national version of the Alaska petroleum fund that gives annual dividends to every citizen.

19. Get tough on corporate crime.

This demand gets the same support, more or less, from the public as the cry to get tough on street crime, especially when the preventable mass casualties stemming from corporate misbehavior is in the mix. What the public see day after day on the corporate-owned news stations is street crime, not crime in the suites. The rule of law, as applicable to both street-level and boardroom-level crime, is a central theme from Adam Smith to Edmund Burke to Friedrich Hayek, all the way to present-day conservative principles.

That this is not clear to many people who are interested in conservative law and order discussions, which focus solely on street-level lawbreaking, is due to the corporatist agenda, which occupies the attention of their affinity think tanks and business-allied opinion makers. The corporatists detour these thinkers by steering their funding trajectories away from any concern with corporate wrongdoing; they absorb them by shifting their focus to abuses committed by trial lawyers or the "enemies of capitalism"; they encourage them to blame the state as the cause of just about everything bad in the world. For these thinkers, there are always steady rewards in terms of contributions, lecture fees, grants, and other incentives for such narrowing of focus.

On top of this, bar associations and the legal profession defend their corporate clients accused of or investigated for possible criminal activities. Meanwhile, the very definition of corporate crime is being blurred by lobbying against criminal penalties in regulatory statutes and shifting any sporadic enforcement into the more lenient arena of civil violations. A fast-growing settlement procedure by the Justice Department known as "deferred prosecution" permits the culpable company to avoid admitting guilt and is excused by the very small enforcement budgets in the Justice Department, which leave officials privately saying they can find no other way to begin to keep up with the corporate crime wave. As reported by the *Corporate Crime Reporter*, they claim not to have the lawyers, prosecutors, and infrastructure to keep tabs on the well-defended companies, who use shareholder assets to pay their expenses. Lacking knowledge of this background, people from all persuasions everywhere cannot see how it is that no major crooks involved in Wall Street's 2008 crash have been prosecuted and sent to jail.

Once some conservative officeholders clear their conscience of unwarranted corporatist inhibitions, and some liberal officeholders stop flirting for the same corporate campaign largesse given to their counterparts, their senses of right and wrong can converge. It will be none too soon, because then the enormous toll our country is paying as a result of corporate toxic harms on people's health and frauds on consumers, investors, pensioners, and the government (e.g., Medicare), in addition to the destabilizing Wall Street and giant bank shenanigans, will be addressed. This liberation of conscience by enough politicians is not likely to occur without the prompting of self-organized communities around the country, who want this marauding at their expense to stop—never mind political labels.

20. Empower the owner-shareholders of public corporations.

Here is the demand that captures, in essence, the direct clash between the corporatists at their pinnacle and the intricately powerless capitalist owners who want to have some control of the company they own shares in, if only to receive an adequate dividend and honest accounting. This desire is quickened when they see their shares fall as the company is mismanaged or strip-mined by vastly overpaid executives, compliments of their well-fed, rubber-stamping board of directors. Here is openly exposed the myth and the farce of the "people's capitalism," written about ad infinitum in the business press and in thoughtful books by authors such as Robert Monks, Nomi Prins, and Jeff Gates. The earlier work by the brilliant team of Adolf Berle and Gardiner Means back in the 1930s showed, with historic documentation, the dire consequences of the separation of formal ownership from executive control within large corporations.

When things are going well with sales, profits, shareholder value, and management, discussion of this separation—so inimical to the basic tenets of capitalism—is muted. It creates little static. Take Apple, for instance, which, until 2012, declined to pay a dividend out of its fast-growing $100 billion cash hoard and, because of rocketing share prices, received little flak from investors over this policy. But when trouble arises, as in the 2008–2009 Wall Street orgy-collapse-bailout, shareholder frustration with shattered or vaporized shares erupts. But it is an eruption without any focus or impact. Just ask the devastated individual and institutional shareholders of Citigroup, Bank of America, Merrill Lynch, Washington Mutual, AIG, Fannie Mae, and Freddie Mac or other former blue chips for confirmation. Their losses were brushed aside. In the power calculus surrounding the wreckage, as negotiations went on between Washington and Wall Street, the common shareholders mattered only tactically in addressing the question of whether the companies would be eliminated totally or allowed to survive badly shrunken, with a small chance to recover a little of their looted assets through their rescued or merged company. Author and corporate lawyer Robert Monks characterizes a system in which shareholders have this impotent status as "capitalism without owners."

There is no clearer view of shareholder impotence exhibited and no clearer analysis of this situation than that of Republican Ben Stein writing about the numerous instances of private equity or investment buyouts of operating companies, often with the collusion of management. Stein is a lawyer and the son of Herbert Stein, who was chair of the Council of Economic Advisers under President Nixon. No more perceptive and ethical critic of Wall Street's abuses has written in the pages of the *New York Times*, the *Wall Street Journal*, and *Barron's Financial Weekly*. In a September 3, 2006, *Times* column titled, "On Buyouts, There Ought to Be a Law," Ben Stein took note of the times in the stock market's corrective process when the asset value of shares is greater than the stock prices. This attracts firms that persuade the managers, with lucrative incentives, to go along with a low-price leveraged buyout. The takeover men then slice and dice the company and multiply what they paid for it many times over. Stein says, "These deals should be illegal on their face . . . as a matter of law."[29]

He gives the following reasons: (1) the assets belong to the shareholders to be managed by their trustee managers as a fiduciary duty to maximize their value; (2) by colluding with outside vulture investors and buying the assets on the cheap, then reaping the personal benefits, the managers are breaching that fiduciary duty and engaging in the ultimate conflict of interest; (3) the lack of disclosure of the memos for the buyout investors, saying how much they expect to make on the deal, hides from the stockholders how much more the assets the new buyers are purchasing are worth (the SEC prohibits withholding such materials); and (4) this secretive, conflicted process reeks of "insider trading" by management.

He winds up with these words: "If the stockholders have hired you (the corporate managers) and pay your wage to manage their assets, your job is to do that for them—not to buy them out at fire-sale prices and turn around and make billions that rightfully belong to them. The management buyout (with other investment banks, private equity firms, etc.) is a sad and infuriating avatar of a decadent age."[30]

Other than by reading the *Wall Street Journal* and the rest of the business press for daily confirmation, does anything more need to be said to show people of all political labels that they share a need to ramp up investor power? All that remains is to propose the strategies that will organize the willing shareholder community (individuals, mutual funds, pension funds, and others) to watchdog their out-of-control, self-enriching hired hands. I have a proposal that can make sure that the investor-protection laws are strengthened and enforced.

My favorite starter idea is to have some former chairs and officials of the Securities and Exchange Commission, and other leading well-known investor power advocates (Robert Monks, John

Bogle, Paul Volcker, Arthur Levitt, William Donaldson, Lynn Turner, and Ben Stein among them), get together to urge shareholders to pledge a voluntary one cent per share per year to fund a company-by-company independent watchdog operation whose full-time staff would directly answer to each company's contributing shareholders group. A mere ten billion shares, out of trillions of outstanding shares, self-assessed one cent per share, would hire a full-time watchdog for each of the top five hundred corporations in the country. Not that hard to get rolling if we had these leaders providing seed money for a group to promote the assessment and going on TV, radio, and the Internet to push for this operation!

Let's get some convergence moving. Conservative and liberal shareholders arise to join this penny brigade! You have nothing to lose but your voiceless power to take hold of the company you own and everything to gain by protecting your share values from decline or collapse, engineered by overpaid or looting management.

The next four areas of convergence concern our health and that of the planet.

21. Ban the patenting of life forms.

This was a call that came from all sides, following the 5–4 Supreme Court decision in 1980 in *Diamond v. Chakrabarty*, which did allow such patents, in this case of a mouse gene. The call has attracted backers from the LC. An initial protest against the patenting of human and other genes came from the Council on Responsible Genetics, started by Harvard and MIT scientists. Both Jeremy Rifkin and Andrew Kimbrell did early work giving cogent reasons to oppose such patenting. Rifkin also reached out to religious leaders, who issued a statement in 1995. In their Joint Appeal against Human and Animal Patenting (1995), these leaders, numbering about one hundred and eighty, "denounced all attempts to patent nature." In the statement, some of the members of the Joint Appeal "compared gene patenting to slavery, while others claimed that gene patents treat human beings as marketable commodities."[31]

Commercializing the world's genetic inheritance—a vastly tumultuous perturbation of Nature—is defended by Monsanto and other biotech companies (all of which have received government subsidies for their research) as providing the proper incentives to companies who will create new products, from food to medicine. The problem is that these rationalizations ignore such serious issues as consent, privacy, safety, profiteering, the possibility of the dangerous migration of engineered seeds, environmental disruption, and what some have called the danger of "playing God."

There has been no legal and ethical framework developed to control this global corporate effort that amounts to changing the nature of nature.[32] The engineering of genes has been rushing along, moving outside the lab into markets and environments far ahead of the science that has to be its governing or restraining discipline. Unlike academic science, the experiments of corporate science are neither peer-reviewed nor done openly. And this for-profit science is obviously a lot more connected to corporate political muscle in Washington, DC, than what is produced in the academies. More than 90 percent of the American people, for example, want labeling on genetically engineered foods sold in the stores. Monsanto disagrees. It is Monsanto that has prevailed over the many, ensuring that this labeling is not required by law.

There is too little convergence muscle here, given the available knowledge necessary to justify immediate efforts and tap into the latent public outrage at this commercial control of our genetic heritage. There is plenty on the record; see the website of the Council for Responsible Genetics (see http://www.councilforresponsiblegenetics .org). Now is the time to go on the ramparts of action to occupy a civic values position in an area where the biotech industry and its supporters are already swarming.

22. Rethink the war on drugs.

This failed program has been drawing serious critiques from both the Left and Right for years. Running from Milton Friedman, William F. Buckley, Jr., Ron Paul, and George Will to former Baltimore mayor and dean of Howard University Law School Kurt Schmoke and legal scholars like Kevin Zeese and numerous judges, the malignant folly of trying to criminalize profitable markets in addictive products has been documented. Decades of lost lives, broken users, broken families, waves of homicides, devastated societies, and violence in other nations, all without denting the overall flow of the products, have woken up thinkers and doers on all sides. Viewing drug addictions as health problems, as they are viewed for addictions manifested by tobacco users and alcoholics, seems the height of prudence, instead of viewing them as crimes whose perpetrators overfill our prisons. The classification and prosecution of drug use as a crime has activated and corrupted law enforcement, encouraged a truly self-defeating form of big government, endangered urban neighborhoods and many thousands of lives, and drained tens of billions of dollars a year from taxpayers. The war on drugs has crowded our overloaded court dockets and given our country the highest incarceration rate per capita of nonviolent offenders in the world. With decriminalization, a portion of these costs can be devoted to humane treatment of addicts, once the addictive products are brought to the surface and regulated in astute ways. We have seen repeatedly that outright prohibition does not work and breeds systems of ever-profitable crimes committed by suppliers and dealers, who produce both official corruption and serious mayhem in maintaining their turfs.

The Left-Right consensus on seeing the criminal justice system as broken is more than verbal and more than recoiling against the excessive cost to taxpayers from locking up so many nonviolent offenders for so long. It has blossomed into a regular reform drive, manifested at the state legislative levels and spreading to the federal prison system. These reforms have not yet affected the abysmal, often sadistic conditions in these crowded prisons. Rather, they are focusing on changing the mandatory-minimum sentencing system that has stripped judges of any discretion and caused a huge arbitrary explosion in the prison population over the past thirty years, even as street crime has declined substantially.

Early on, conservative Chuck Colson, a former special assistant to President Nixon and a former inmate, having been convicted as a result of the Watergate scandal, sounded the drums against the incarceration reflex—lock 'em up and throw the keys away—through his prison ministry. Other conservatives now favoring proven approaches toward rehabilitation, education, and prevention include former Reagan attorney general Ed Meese, former congressman Asa Hutchinson, Republican Party mass mailing pioneer Richard A. Viguerie, "ethics czar" William Bennett, and, the *Washington Monthly* reported, "even the now-infamous American Legislative Exchange Council" (ALEC). These efforts, the *Monthly* avers, give political cover to Democrats terrified of appearing soft on crime before voters.[33]

Of course the longtime work on rational criminal enforcement, incarceration, and prevention policies by groups such as the ACLU, the NAACP, the Open Society Foundations, and the Public Welfare Foundation is made easier with such operating convergence or even parallel, separate efforts.

Presently, the leadership of increasing numbers of Right and Left state legislators is passing juvenile justice legislation replacing draconian law with constructive interventionist programs of education, training, close counseling, and due process to reduce incarceration. Further, states like California (SB 26) are now passing legislation that gives prisoners who committed crimes as adolescents an opportunity to work toward lower sentences if they can demonstrate remorse and rehabilitative behavior. These laws are receiving support from police chiefs, sheriffs, district attorneys, and judges who would call themselves conservatives.

The waves of change are touching Congress. The federal criminal justice and prison system has been sharply criticized by Attorney General Eric Holder as "broken." In August 2013, Mr. Holder declared "too many Americans go to too many prisons for far too long, and for no truly good law-enforcement reason."[34] He has proposed reforms, many of them similar to successful enactments made a few years ago by arch right-winger and Texas governor Rick Perry.

The facts overwhelmingly back up Mr. Holder's criticisms. The *Economist* reports that "drug offenders are nearly half of all federal prisoners, and most people convicted of federal drug offences received mandatory-minimum sentences." Possessing five grams of crack cocaine requires a sentence of five years in prison for a first-time offender. From 1980 the federal prison population has increased nearly tenfold, going from 24,000 inmates to 219,000 inmates, while the violent crime rate is one-third lower than what it was in 1982 and less than half that in 1997.[35]

An unprecedented alliance of Left-Right and Middle is building around the demand of "no more drug war." A full-page notice in the *New York Times* on December 20, 2012, asserted that "we strive for the day when drug policies are no longer motivated by ignorance, fear and prejudice but rather by science, compassion, fiscal prudence and human rights, with education and treatment available for everyone."[36] It featured a Drug Policy Alliance Honorary Board ranging from former chair of the Federal Reserve Paul Volcker to former attorneys general, cabinet secretaries, mayors, and judges.

There is a long trek ahead, however. In March 2013, Senator Patrick Leahy, chair of the Senate Judiciary Committee and the new senator Rand Paul introduced the Justice Safety Valve Act of 2013, allowing judges to impose sentences below mandatory minimums. This joint Democratic–Republican filing needs far more public mobilization if it is to be more than just a filing and a joint press release. But the groundswell is at least visible on the horizon. As conservative George Will described in his column, "they hope to reduce the cruelty, irrationality and cost of the current regime of mandatory minimum sentences for federal crimes."[37]

Driving such a groundswell is the National Campaign to Reform State Juvenile Justice Systems, which works daily with twenty state-based efforts "to provide strategic resources to end the reliance on punitive responses toward juvenile crime and delinquency and move toward evidence-based rehabilitative and restorative approaches. Founded by large nonprofit institutes, led by the MacArthur Foundation and super-organizer Donald K. Ross, the effort, supported active campaigns in eighteen states by 2013 and retained twenty-five lobbying firms and other support structures. Mr. Ross crisply asserts that legislative successes in state after state embody Left-Right alliances inside and outside state legislatures.

This subject has already called up enough polemical fervor on both sides for convergence, but it will take more than that to lift the heavily policed hand of government so as to replace our current drug war with a much smarter set of public policies. Here convergence, once it gets underway, will tap deeply into the historical philosophies of conservatism and liberalism. (See the documentary *The House I Live In* at http://www.thehouseilivein.org.)

23. Prioritize the protection of our environment.

The need for ecological consciousness to preserve the planet Earth and its posterity seems to be common sense. Instead, it viscerally divides Republicans and Democrats. Thank the Republicans in Congress for desiring to close out the EPA and OSHA in a corporatist-encouraged rage, an example of truly ignorant nihilism. The science and evidence of climate change and global warming are casualties of this rejectionism. Senator James Inhofe (R-OK) repeatedly calls global warming one of the greatest hoaxes of the century. He does not say it's exaggerated or partially erroneous, but a hoax—something completely made up.

Many self-described conservatives do show little care for the environment, that is, except when they are outdoors with their families as tourists. This is at least partially based in partisanship, since they insist on attaching the liberal or Democrat label to the occasional governmental initiatives to enforce the environmental laws, the ones that so anger industry.

Still, earlier conservatives often embraced environmentalism. In the appendix to his book *Conservatism Revisited*, written in 1974, Peter Viereck called the young people in the early seventies who were marching and acting for environmental protection "unconsciously conservative . . . even when under radical slogans," as they protested "against what [Herman] Melville called 'the impieties of progress.'"[38] Today when we are beset by such problems as recessions, wars, bailouts, and credit crises, it may not seem to some to be a good political climate for working on ecological advancement or even for staying the course to avert us from sliding ecologically backwards for lack of public investment and regulatory compliance. But for considering the possibility of convergence in tough times, like now, a little looking backward is a good start.

If there were ever an argument to be made on the importance of historical knowledge, it could be made by looking back at the Republicans' heritage as a way of cutting through the ideas of the present self-styled Republican conservatives in Congress and other elected officials, who stand adamantly against most environmental and consumer regulations. It's as if they didn't recognize that they too are breathers, drinkers, eaters, and motorists!

Our first historical lesson is to remember that the conservation movement against despoilment of land, air, and water started in a big way with President Theodore Roosevelt and his fellow

Republicans. Over a hundred years ago, they were the activists who established the national forests, the great national parks, and other reserves for posterity to enjoy.

Other than through an extension of their nineteenth-century belief in the need for husbandry of our resources and from biblical wisdom, where did they get such foresight and such a sense of the necessity—not just pleasure—of the communion between nature and the human spirit? It helped, of course, that they had a lot of land and beauty available, having wrested it from the Native Americans. But critical also was the legacy of conservative philosophers, who preached a conservation ethic and had a sense of holding a public trust for those who followed them. Perhaps not always explicit, these were the views that animated Roosevelt's doers from Gifford Pinchot to John Muir and that maintained a lasting influence, though more diminished, right down to the Nixon administration.

Under President's Nixon's tenure, the Democrats and Republicans in Congress passed the major environmental laws of our generation, bolstered by his signature and eloquent supporting statements. Besides being deeply impressed (or alarmed) by the massive, all-American turnout for Earth Day in 1970, Nixon also knew that poll after poll showed Republicans themselves favored saving the natural world from plunder and pollution. He was reading both the philosophic and pragmatic tea leaves. It was absurd to keep soiling our own nests!

About this time, Russell Kirk, a grand savant of modern conservatism, was writing that "the issue of environmental quality is one which transcends traditional political boundaries. It is a cause which can attract, and very sincerely, liberals, conservatives, radicals, reactionaries, freaks and middle class straights."[39] Recently, John Gray, the British political philosopher, declared, "Far from having a natural home on the Left, concern for the integrity of the common environment, human as well as ecological, is most in harmony with the outlook of traditional conservatism of the British and European varieties."[40] To which Mr. Kirk added, "Nothing is more conservative than conservation."[41]

These and other ecumenical judgments should not be surprising. Common human biological inheritances and an aesthetic appreciation of nature transcend ideologies. People naturally want health, safety, and beauty. They want nature to last and be bountiful. They do not abide pain, filth, and having their children and grandchildren degraded and deprived of the memories they or their grandparents and great-grandparents had when rivers, streams, and lakes were there to enjoy and forests were there to explore.

All these commonalities did not go unnoticed by the corporatists, for whom nature was to be exploited for profit or off-loaded to cut costs. They had become accustomed to using our air, water, soil, and natural patrimony as free goods or, some would say, free sewers for disposing wastes and emissions into our biosphere. They did not want to invest and internalize the monies that would be needed to be spent for safe disposal or reuse or to drop unsafe procedures altogether. Suddenly, within two years (1970–1972), they were confronted by federal and state laws that told them they no longer would be the sole deciders in how fatally toxic the human environment would be either outside (the Environmental Protection Agency) or in the workplace (Occupational Safety and Health Administration). This legislation came with an awakened public consciousness that change was overdue, necessary, and urgent. Fully twenty million people participated for at least a few hours in their communities during the weeklong celebration of Earth Day in 1970. The mass media widely headlined this historic civic event.

Presently, the networking of convergence in relation to environmental pursuits comes when an occurrence in any locality threatens neighborhoods, which face the danger in common, untroubled by competing economic interests. Lois Gibbs, inspired by her grim experience during the 1970s raising her family unknowingly over the toxic soil of Love Canal, New York, created a national grassroots environmental group in 1981 that organized thousands of small communities threatened by such problems as toxic leaks into their basements and drinking water or gaseous fumes around their homes and schools. She says that, whether during her visits to polluted "hot spots" or during her large convocations, which draw grassroots activists from around the country to Washington, DC, she does not detect any ideological divide. The people working with her are activists. They want healthful conditions for their children, and they want polluters to stop, laws to be enforced, courtroom doors to be opened, and honest disclosures to be made about environmental conditions. Common threats invite common ground.

On the other hand, sailing is not so smooth when there are severe local controversies over competing material interests that do not break down by political persuasion. The struggle to end mountaintop removal by people in the Appalachian hollows pits the downstream people against the coal companies, their suppliers, and a dwindling supply of workers. The burgeoning struggle over natural gas fracking is another case. Communities have also been riven when a large corporate project, such as a new nuclear power plant, entices a locality with property tax reductions, thus solidifying supporters against others who fear the risks of radioactive leaks and accidents and taxpayer bailouts more than they desire any short-term advantages.

On more macro-environmental disputes, such as over global warming or acid rain, ideologies become divisive. These disputes feature the different groupings presenting pro and con regulatory actions or proposals. "Big Government" and "Big Business" accusations come into play here, with the sides accusing each other of promoting one or the other.

Convergence is needed here, particularly in decision-making forums like Congress, where systemic decisions would have to be made. There, however, the division between Republicans and Democrats has hardened to a point that proactive politicians worried about global warming have become mostly silent. They have made the calculation that a subdued attitude loses fewer voters than a clarion call for action that their opposition—the deniers—can tie to incurring huge taxpayer and consumer expenditures for what, the deniers still assert, is an unsubstantiated prediction. The climate change believers marvel at how, by manipulating propaganda, the deniers have swayed a sizable segment of public opinion. Yet those worried about warming have made little attempt themselves to publicize, with supportive companies, including the insurance industry, the persuasive rebuttals that exist of these deniers' ideas, such as the one by energy expert and long-time converger Amory Lovins. He shows that conversion from fossil fuels and nuclear power to renewables and conservation efficiencies will be a profitable investment for society, save consumers money, save on taxes, create more jobs, advance national security, and generate a safer environment for communities and workers. Yet the "Inhofing"—Senator James Inhofe is a blatant anthropogenic climate change denier—of public opinion continues unabated among conservatives, even as evidence piles up about the reality of global warming, including a 2004 Pentagon study,[42] which concluded that the coming climate change from human activities constitutes a major national security risk.

As we've seen, this entire subject is infused with both economic interests and ideologies. That makes for a volatile cocktail. At the moment it is particularly inimical to attracting convergence. However, as the visual and empirical evidence mounts, the foreboding and storming reality may start to dissolve the hardened congressional opposition that is stalling a nation's organized sense of the need for precautions and remedies.

On the ground, events can move more quickly. In Arizona, Barry Goldwater Jr., son of Mr. Conservative, has formed an organization opposed to monopoly electric utilities trying to "extinguish" rooftop solar installations by reducing credits for excess solar power transferred to the utility. To Goldwater and Tea Party groups, the issue is greater consumer choice.

24. Advance health.

Health, as distinguished from insurance or health care, is as perfect an objective process for local convergence as anything. A concise description of the possibilities was expressed in 2008 by Dr. Julie L. Gerberding, then director of the Centers for Disease Control and Prevention, in a letter to the *Wall Street Journal*:

> Right now, 75% of our current health expenditures target treatment for preventable conditions caused by tobacco use, poor diet and inactivity, alcohol and drug use, motor-vehicle crashes, firearms and other risks. It's time to broaden our conversation about reform to include the entire health system. Public health agencies, businesses, community groups, teachers, and above all, parents have a strong stake in our success.[43]
>
> We have to promote changes and policies that build health opportunities into everyday life: walkable streets, nutritious school lunches, health education and fitness programs for all students, smoking-cessation programs and easy access to parks and gyms.
>
> The Centers for Disease Control and Prevention is in full support of a rapidly expanding movement to help America become the "healthiest nation."

I've never heard Rep. Ron Paul call for the abolition of the Centers for Disease Control, a government agency. Its mission cannot be controversial except for those bent on not being deterred from masochism or suicide. Whenever those flu viruses come from overseas—so far, primarily from the Chinese mainland to America—all eyes are on these Centers. Their scientists and public health experts have no axe to grind, and focus on saving lives and heading off diseases and injuries.

Now why does this red, white, and blue, all-American desire for good health need to be considered an endeavor for convergence? Don't people work together every day in hometown USA, regardless of their political partisanship, to help people either as paid specialists or as volunteers? Look at all the YMCAs, volunteer fire departments, social programs at churches, Big Brother/Big Sister programs, service clubs, and organized exercise events.

Well, it might also be asked: Why is convergence needed to overcome when there is no opposition? Who in these fifty states is opposed to better health practices? Ah, it is the intangibles and the impersonals.

First, contrary to Dr. Gerberding's hopes and those of the First Lady Michelle Obama, we do not see a "rapidly expanding movement" to improve health. True, there is some positive news (more backyard gardens), and there is some negative news (high levels of obesity, malnutrition, and diseases like diabetes). But overall, much more needs to be done everywhere and every day to increase engagement with the issue. Such a personal, people-intensive change of lifestyles, opting for a healthier way of existing, may be brought about by ads or urgings from on high. But there is nothing like the support of your friends, neighbors, and extended relatives, and having community facilities where you live, work, and play as a way to provide the regular camaraderie and intensity millions of Americans need to overcome seductive TV ads that lead to bad health. School administrators who don't understand the need to restore physical education class, as well as the culture of sedentary living, junk food/drink, and the addictive things so many consume or inhale, need this ground-level consistent rejection.

Because the desire for health is shared among everyone, it is something that can be used to break down the artificial social divisions that separate those of different political convictions. Let's face it, even though millions of LC people are cordial to one another in many settings daily, there is a remarkable self-segregation socially and civically. People just like to spend time with people who have similar likes and dislikes. Differing views or experiences on guns, abortion, school prayer, smoking, school busing (more in the past), foreign wars, home schooling, local political party differences, affirmative action, the poor, and issues subject to local voting, as well as the questions of volunteerism and taxes, tend to stratify whom people choose to spend time with year in and year out. At the extremes, animosities may erupt, which permanently etch the so-called red/blue demarcation.

If such people come together, the ones who are usually confronting each other, in order to advance the cause of promoting healthier lives for adults and their children, new energy will emerge to fortify these transformations. It is worth making a big deal when local residents, known for being adversarial, are converging. Certainly bureaucrats, who are accustomed to their set patterns, when they see such bipartisan convergence, will realize that doing little or nothing is not acceptable to the whole spectrum of their service area. Bureaucratic inertia loses its easy excuse when it is no longer faced by a divided community.

To facilitate convergence, there are very fine and interesting videos, pamphlets, posters, contests, authority figures (e.g., athletes), and how-to's for marathons, all free, available at your fingertips on the Internet. A profusion of recent apps—some also free—facilitate micro-monitoring of one's progress, though none will be better than what the locals can think up for themselves.

Imagine a poster with pictures of two polarized community leaders with the caption, "We're together on this drive for quality health and longer life, because our teams want to keep fighting each other for many more years." Such collaboration doesn't preclude contests, a favorite way to motivate as urged by famed anthropologist Margaret Mead. Think of a contest on this question: Can conservative families lose weight more safely than liberal families? Many permutations on this theme can be envisioned. They may be funny, corny, hilarious—so what, if they motivate?

There is an additional collateral benefit. The two opposites meet and work together. They experience "the other." They discover broader and deeper dimensions to their humanity. They discover that the other possesses skills and activities not stereotypically associated with a holder of such political attitudes. From there, they start proposing other community projects they wish to see accomplished. Pretty soon they start questioning or resisting the self-serving authority figures above them at the state and national level in politics and through the media whose careers rely on manipulating by simplification, distortion, and sometimes dissembling. All in all, productive serendipities come over the horizon. There is less looking at screens night and day. Fulfillment of other human possibilities beckon!

The last point is in a category all by itself.

25. *Diffuse convergence.*

Speaking of grand visions, after a few successful convergent missions, careful consideration should be given to finding donors to establish an Institute for the Advancement of Convergence, whose mission would be the diffusing of convergence itself. As one of the architects of the European Common Market, Jean Monnet, wrote, "Nothing is possible without men but without institutions nothing is lasting."[44] After the charitable jobs projects, convergers will have made contact with many wealthy people and foundations. Surely a few of them would have become excited enough over these collaborations to fund such an institute that jump-starts and accelerates this huge, untapped potential for individual and societal betterment.

6

Obstacles to Convergence and How to Overcome Them

Ten Obstacles to Conservatives Working for Convergence

Time for crossover empathy. First let's look into the mind of a conservative leader, opinion maker, or other paid careerist who upholds the faith. You would like to work openly with your liberal/progressive counterparts on any number of contemporary outrages, abuses, power plays, and affronts to conservative principles. The foregoing pages provided numerous examples from this menu. What mental checklist would you have to consult before deciding whether to make a serious public entry into an arena where you would join with those of a different ideological perspective?

There are ten to contemplate, at the very least.

First, ask: Would you jeopardize your funding by joining forces to take on a deplorable corporate practice or position? Whether you work at a think tank, a university, a corporate law firm, a public relations firm, or as an independent consultant, you would have to think twice. Money from businesses, their foundations, and their executives flow daily into these institutions' coffers. If they

121

are not overtly contractual, the implied quid pro quo in exchange
for this largesse is that the donor will get a polemical or scholarly
defense to trumpet to third parties. When the big box chains want
to block minimum wage increases, even those that just keep up
with inflation, they draw on their scholarly apologists to "demonstrate conclusively" that such raises will cost lower-paid workers
their jobs. Walmart, McDonald's, and Pizza Hut spokespeople are
not as convincing on these topics as "Professor Deliver" or the
Cato Institute or the Hoover Institution.

The late Paul Weyrich, a founder of resurgent political conservatism with populist features in Washington, DC, received corporate grants for his groups from "Amoco, General Motors, Chase
Manhattan Bank, and right-wing foundations like Olin and Brad-
ley," according to William Greider. Typically, Mr. Weyrich was
forthright, telling Greider: "We have to co-exist with these people
[the Republican fundraisers] because if they put out the word that
you're not reliable, your contributors will go away."[1]

Second, you may find your plate is full, and you're behind on
all kinds of publishing deadlines, preparation for testimonies, expert witnessing, litigation loads, conferences to be attended, and
faraway lectures to be given. You may find you just don't have any
time to take on a new experience in which you will be receiving unaccustomed denunciations and rebuttals to which you are
obliged to spend time responding.

Third, you find that there is no infrastructure supporting your
bold ventures. What work you do has always been within your
existing infrastructure, which has long-standing, defined expectations for you.

Your servicers, colleagues, superiors, and interns are part of
your workplace, with its common thinking and settled assessments
of each other. It is uncomfortable to go off the chart. When I in-
terviewed former Judge Andrew Napolitano on C-SPAN in 2011
about his new book *It Is Dangerous to Be Right When the Government
Is Wrong*, he forcefully declared that George W. Bush and Dick

Cheney should be criminally prosecuted by Attorney General Eric Holder for their war crimes in Iraq and Afghanistan. "What are you waiting for, Attorney General Holder?" he exclaimed. Earlier on the program, he said that Bush and Cheney should have been impeached by Congress for multiple violations of the Constitution, starting with their flouting of the Congress's war-declaring authority. Mr. Napolitano then returned to his employer Fox News, where he had made regular television appearances and received some cold stares and mutterings of disapproval. Freedom of speech was still a tolerated virtue, so Napolitano survived, especially since he had written numerous books that demonstrated his knowledge and sincerity on constitutionalism. But what if he had gone the next step and bunkered with advocates of his position so as to take speech toward action, as did Fox's Glenn Beck with his passions? It is doubtful that the judge would just be getting stares in retaliation for his position.

Fourth, your social life might shut down. Invitations to homes and restaurants for dinner start to decline. You're not on the guest list anymore. Outings with your customary friends and their families become rarer. Your deviation from the norm is seen as apostasy or blasphemy. A few tough-skinned conservatives may shrug this off. Most are hurt and cannot easily abide ostracism.

Fifth, if you're anticipating job mobility, forget it when you show you really mean to stand tall against corporate power. Once you act on your convictions, you're not seen as reliable enough to be given offers of high-paying jobs and well-paid lectures in the corporate sector or to receive moonlighting consultancies to amplify your regular income, which you believe doesn't match your versatile talents. What's more, certain angry companies with aggressive CEOs will affirmatively try to make you and your organization personae non gratae.

The lives of conservative corporate employees whose consciences turned them into whistle-blowers and who joined the opposition to the tobacco, nuclear, drug, and other industries have been difficult, to put it mildly. Would-be convergers take due notice of what happens to these conscientious people. Being "blacklisted" is terrifying, in particular to long-time corporate employees used to no other livelihood. This is especially the case if they are specialized and cannot draw on other commensurate skills for their livelihood.

Sixth, you might ask yourself: Why not satisfy yourself by making a studious gesture that implies it will go no further? Kind of having your cake and eating it too, but not really.

One of my favorite illustrations of this type of "thinking twice" happened in 2001, when public reports condemning corporate welfare and subsidies of various kinds were put out by the Heritage Foundation and the Cato Institute.[2] On hearing this good news, I looked forward to the think tanks' next steps and admired their courage in the face of who was funding them. After all, Heritage, for one, has never been squeamish about sending staffers up to Capitol Hill, where they work to produce public hearings and transform the agendas of their legislative allies in a business-friendly direction. No one can forget how much they did in this regard the moment Ronald Reagan became president in 1981.

Well, very little followed the scathing reports against corporate welfare. The two conservative think tanks did not retract their views and continued occasionally to repeat their displeasure. They just did not extend this to more forceful advocacy levels. They managed, however, to achieve public credibility for taking positions contrary to much of the corporate world, which is on welfare of one sort or another. (This includes Silicon Valley.) This reputation, in turn, redounded to the advantage of the outside corporate lobbyists, who daily cloak their over-the-edge profiteering with "legitimizing" reports and studies by these well-endowed institutions.

Seventh, a popular rationalization for thinking twice was brought to my attention by Fred Smith, the long-standing libertarian head of the Center for a Competitive Enterprise. "Ralph," he said, "it isn't that we don't agree on the goals—health, safety, economic well-being and so on. It is that we disagree on the means of getting there." He said this in the context of our conversation as to why more convergence does not happen between LC groups in Washington, DC. Fred may be correct as far as he goes. But he may be thinking twice, since he is ignoring partial opportunities that cannot be so easily dismissed by referring to the means-ends conflict. So there is disagreement about means to ends. Well, what about, as a start, agreeing on procedures, such as insisting on due process; disclosure of government information; ending the Fast Track, no-amendment procedure for ramming trade agreements through Congress; or ending the frequent e-mail–sufficient notice for filibustering in the Senate? Senator Mitch McConnell sends an email to Senate Majority Leader Democrat Harry Reid indicating there may be "extended debate." To Reid, that means if he doesn't have sixty votes, McConnell blocks any bill going to the Senate floor for a vote.

As for the means/ends problem, what are we to make of this counterintuitive recognition by Arthur Brooks, president of the right-wing, neocon, corporatist American Enterprise Institute (AEI), writing in the *Washington Post* in 2011? Following a predictable screed about limited government and the "fairness" nonsense, he delivered these concise words:

> There is certainly a role for government in this system. Private markets can fail due to monopolies (which eliminate competition), externalities (such as pollution), the need for public goods (such as education, which is indispensable in an opportunity society), corruption and crime. Furthermore, most economists agree that some social safety net is appropriate in a civilized society. When the government focuses on these things, it assists the free enterprise system.[3]

No doubt on his last point, but Mr. Brooks does leave open the possibility of disagreement over what government means are best to work toward the goals he espouses for a "civilized society."

However, as for thinking twice, neither he nor the AEI—a large organization—has backed government antitrusters, environmental enforcers, crackdowns on corporate crimes, or the public Social Security and Medicare safety nets, which he seems to allude to in his article. Overwhelmingly, his active sensibilities have reflected piles of AEI reports demanding deregulation, the privatizing of government safety nets, and going along with big military budgets as well as tolerating endemic business fraud in Medicare, Medicaid, and other areas.

Thinking twice may also explain the actions of William Bennett, author of the big best seller *The Book of Virtues*, for a time the very definer and popular exponent of conservative values. In the nineties he was regaled by all in conservative circles, paid handsomely for lectures by many, and challenged for his orthodoxy by none. The man wrote *the* book on American cultural virtues: history, homestead, business, and religious foundations. I called him one day, having made his acquaintance earlier through his famous Washington corporate lawyer brother, Bob, who once jokingly accused me of sending him so many defendants that he paid his childrens' college tuition with the fees he collected. "Bill," I asked, "would you agree that corporate power is on a collision course with conservative principles?" Without hesitation, he replied, "Yes."

Since that exchange years ago, I kept wondering why he did not take the next steps. Why has he not led the way, defending his revered life philosophy and those who share it from damage, diminishment, and contamination by the omnipresent forces of commercialism and immoral manipulative marketing to adults and their children? A few sporadic appearances against commercial exploitation of children are not enough, given his stature and media recognition. There are reasons for thinking twice that are unfathomable. The Bill Bennett puzzle is one of them. I'll leave it at that!

Eighth, some conservative leaders think twice because of a larger disagreement with the other side that spills over into a reluctance to converge where they do agree unequivocally. In an e-mail to me, Ed Crane, the head of the Cato Institute, said it crisply:

> I'm anti-corporatist but anti-statist first. You have it the other way around. Almost all the dishonesty and damage put forward by corporations is facilitated, indeed made possible, by the state. . . .
>
> The Great Recession is primarily the fault of national planners who wanted to make every American a homeowner. The Community Reinvestment Act, Freddie, Fannie, HUD, easy Fed money and trillions of dollars of mal-investment caused by the government created this mess, Ralph. It's not the corporations, it's the government.
>
> We oppose all corporate subsidies. . . . So we also agree on unconstitutional wars, the Patriot Act, and the Fed run amuck. . . . Finally, I prefer the First Amendment to having the government control advertising to kids, adults or pets.
>
> As a matter of fact, I think the alliance you are seeking is not between free market conservatives/libertarians and progressives, but between populist conservatives and progressives. There is a lot in common.[4]

Credit Ed Crane for putting a lot of judgments in a few short sentences. Clearly, we have chicken or egg differences about whether it is government or organized business that is largely the prime initiating culprit. Even so, it might be worthwhile to say a little more about the validity of his arguments.

On many planes the government is a corporate government. At or around the helms of the most powerful departments and agencies reign high officials right out of the business establishment or very close to it. Think of the Treasury Department, the Department of Defense, the Department of Commerce, and the Department of the Interior as evidence. Huge business lobbies know the government is the many-splendored provider of corporate welfare and enormous tax escapes, while showing a willingness to adopt weak, under-funded regulations and offering huge contracts. The corporations are the seekers. Is it permissible to conclude that it's mostly cor-poratism, not the state, that is responsible for the big-ticket items? Even concerning unconstitutional wars, would the White House have invaded Iraq if the defense and related industries seriously objected as corporate citizens, instead of funding neocons and si-lently smacking their lips? Corporations have their own ideological imperatives; governments, such as ours, are not of themselves very ideologically driven. Nevertheless, neither the government, which is full of corporate executives on leave in government positions, nor its elected members, who take campaign cash from corporate PACs, are innocent. They know very well what agenda they're driving. Still, if Mr. Crane says that once the honeypot is spotted or the gold rush begins, then the state provides the goodies, he is right. But we can ask from our side: Who started the merry-go-round, spotted the honeypot, and led the prospectors?

As for his reference to Freddie and Fannie, true, these were started by the federal government, but with the hearty and po-litically hefty approval of the home builders and realtors. Then, years later, they were privatized with public shareholders on the New York Stock Exchange and ended by developing a legendary lobbying muscle over Congress, possessed of all the usual indicia of big companies: stock options, high executive pay based on cooking the books, and every customary behavior and incentive known to Wall Street, right down to powerless investors. Where else could the giant Wall Street banks, that fostered by far most of the risky debt, find such congenial and compatible fall guys for their toxic paper during the subprime mortgage mania? Sure, Fannie and Freddie had an implied backup by the federal government. But so did the Wall Street banks, as we found out in 2008–2009.

Very little is done in Washington, including formulating many but not all the regulations that affect corporations, that is not rewarding to or watered down by Big Business and its lobbyists, many of whom come from congressional or executive branch positions to cash in their know-how and know-who. Obviously, the moment taxpayer debt became an endless magnet for exploitation while the bankers' Federal Reserve was printing money and, now, lending massive sums to the major banks for near zero interest, it could be said that Wall Street had corrupted Washington, making it the possessor of a deficit-driving accounts receivable fund as well as being a last-resort bailout servant. Can anyone think the state started this dynamic? Business tied to greed and power misbehaved long before Big Government started, all the way back to the time when the principal activity and personnel of the federal government were centered on delivering the mail. By the way, the mail service was another early and productive subsidy to business.

In bringing up unconstitutional wars, the PATRIOT Act, and the Fed, in bringing these up, Mr. Crane is iterating a long-standing area of concurrence between Left and Right, but one from which no operating convergence has emerged to combat these seminal ongoing violations and aggravations of what he would call our constitutional republic. Even though these areas of compatibility exist, there is still no move by either side for convergence, though at least the Cato Institute does invite all sides to their luncheon debates and, contrary to strict free market dogma, proves that there is such a thing as a free lunch.

Crane's suggestion that the alliance sought is not with free market conservatives and libertarians but with populist conservatives is an idea that has deep roots, which I'll explore in the next chapter. Suffice it to say that our differences still allow for overlaps, such as the three major examples given by Mr. Crane.

To add to the confusion about the categories, Grover Norquist told me that "the Populist Right likes the PATRIOT Act," and they like public "funding of their favorite baseball stadium." Even so, he allowed that "there are some very real and large areas where principled conservatives and libertarians and progressive critics of corporate statism can work together. He listed "civil liberties . . . the Patriot Act, opposition to bailouts of Wall Street, Fannie Mae, Freddie Mac, etc., government contracting abuses (lack of transparency) and no government funding of baseball/football parks."

As noted, though, often certain basic differences between Left and Right outlooks seem to freeze conservatives, who will not work with liberals, even when there is an avowed similarity of interest concerning certain issues. The same is true for many liberal activists and writers.

Ninth, LC convergence is nobody's top priority or not one that is weighty enough to elicit the effort needed to secure staff, meet, plan, and iron out how far the convergence will go when the heat starts or how to respond when the details start filling in and stumbling blocks arise. It is just so much easier to devote careers to working with like-minded people from the get-go, folks who do not have the baggage of still being your adversaries on many other directions. Intuitively, a conservative sees that as sufficient reason to think twice. Moreover, their work cup is always full.

Tenth, incipient convergent rebellions get crushed, deferred, or punished by their respective leaders. This happened in 2011 to rank-and-file House Republicans and Democrats who viewed President Obama's attack on Libya to be clearly unconstitutional. They were certainly accurate in that conclusion. Mr. Obama asked for neither a declaration of war nor a war resolution; he did not obey the existing 1973 War Resolution Act nor receive an authorization or appropriation of funds for the military action's costs. This bipartisan alliance wanted a vote on a resolution by Rep. Dennis Kucinich (D-OH) requiring the president to withdraw from the Libya operation within fifteen days.

The Kucinich resolution had surprising support, as reported by the press, at the closed-door House Republican Caucus meeting in June 2011. Alarmed, the Republican leaders quickly moved to squelch the resistance, knowing, of course, that the Democratic leaders would not object to their stopping it. A leader of the rebellion, Republican Walter Jones, had his seat on the House Armed Services Committee taken away.

The Fate of Convinced Conveners

Bruce Fein, a prominent, Harvard-educated, constitutional lawyer who had been a deputy assistant attorney general in the Reagan administration, is the ultimate converger. Without any agenda, he tirelessly promotes the due process rule of law and constitutional adherence that preserve the checks and balances in the federal government. For years he has been litigating, writing, and authoring materials on these themes (see http://www.intelcommission .org). As a volunteer adviser to both Republicans and Democrats in Congress, Fein has testified more than two hundred times before congressional committees. Yet, instead of becoming more influential, he has been increasingly marginalized except for his pro bono representation of the father of Edward Snowden in mid-2013. Many of his compelling op-eds and letters to the editor pile up largely unpublished. I have read a number of these responses to contrary editorials or opinion pieces. They are to the point— maybe too much to the point. Recently, his newly formed convergent nonprofit, the National Commission on Intelligence and Foreign Wars, has been unsuccessfully asking for funds from like-minded affluent individuals, who apparently imagine retaliations if they became involved with such collaborations.

Unlike Fein, neocons like Donald Rumsfeld, Paul Wolfowitz, and Douglas Feith, who were wrong legally, morally, and strategically on brutally invading Iraq, and wrong on the costly, spreading imperial aggressions of the US government under both parties, are on the paid lecture trail, receive lucrative book deals, and are welcomed on the op-ed pages of the *New York Times* and *Washington*

Post. One of them, John Bolton, whose war mongering and State Department mischief placed him at odds with his superior, Secretary Colin Powell (who once told me he could not stand Bolton's fatuous belligerence), got different op-eds in the *Times* and the *Post* on the same day—an unheard of coterminous acceptance.

Anyone in a position of some power who might be prone to pursue converging initiatives against the grain will look over such contrasts as that between Bolton and Fein and do a mental cost-benefit calculation that can indispose them to follow such initiatives. This is especially true when most of the media, programmed to limit their attention to covering clashing antagonists who are perceived as having power, rarely see start-up convergences as worthy of reporting to their audiences and readership around the country. Thus, seeds of convergence, no matter how momentous and no matter if they are planted right on Capitol Hill, have less chance of sprouting.

Why Liberals Often Fight Shy of Convergence

The liberal think tanks and advocacy groups are not without their own inhibitions. They have their reasons or excuses, ones that overlap with the foregoing list, for thinking twice. Some parallel those of their conservative counterparts: peer pressure against insidious associations with antagonistic groups and concern over their funders and key allies. The latter point may surprise readers, but bear in mind that liberal organizations receive funding from many foundations with corporate-connected boards of directors or from large donors, who may, for instance, like environmental causes but not any wayward alliances on tax loopholes, trade policies, specific foreign policies, investor power, corporate subsidies, or corporate crimes.

Small donors mainly expect a consistency of opposition to "darker forces" and might not find convergence to their taste either.

After all, don't the fundraising letters they receive feed on that expectation? Other liberal groups have one-issue orientations, with members who expect adherence to that one issue only. On the other hand, single-issue groups, such as opponents of nuclear power, can more easily converge with conservative organizations, which share their focus—ones, for instance, that are opposed to government subsidies and guarantees, a convergence we saw took place in the anti–Breeder Reactor victory. Moreover, there are liberal writers who may agree with some convergence but reject it overall as a bad strategy because they do not want to give any credibility whatsoever to the ad hoc convergent partners from the Right.

Routes to Convergence

I've observed at close hand these restraints over the years and have tried, with limited success, to overcome some of them by urging that the overall reform must be kept in mind. I tell possible joiners of the convergence movement that there is no need to compromise or weaken their position. To create a convergence that will work and endure, at the onset those from the Left should have a take-us-or-leave-us stance, indicating they are not ready to compromise their principles but will work with any good-faith conservative who shares this one goal. This is what the other, conservative side would want for themselves as well.

Ask the Cato Institute's willing, veteran, free market conservative/libertarian Ed Crane about prospects for convergence, and he replies, "Alas, it ain't happening." What Mr. Crane is reflecting is the fundamental polarization between two political-civic forces arrayed against each other over perceived contrasting public and moral philosophies about how the world should conduct itself from the top all the way down to communities and neighborhoods. The worldviews have been bundled into starkly contrary images that come out of our educational, literary, economic, and political systems. Crane seems to recognize that any alliances based on avoiding these rigid binary mentalities can deplete customary emotional mentalities, unsettle strong views, and upset a person's balance, which can only be maintained by adherence to the images.

The escape from this constricting matrix of demarcation can possibly be found in an organizational change. Take staff and resources from existing multi-issue convergers, which have agreed to merge their strength, and move them to a separate new organization or task force where the convergent mission is their only one. This separation, this spinoff, would help the staff shed many of the inhibitions that keep convergence from happening. A similar organizational approach would serve donors who wish to start or support new groups "without the baggage" of old Left-Right conflicts.

Even though corporate welfare has been denounced by the Progressive Policy Institute, Common Cause, Heritage, and Cato—in detail and more than once—individually these groups have gone nowhere because their focus is not on that issue. Were they to join resources, apply for additional ones, and start a new advocacy entity devoted singularly to opposing and discrediting this massive redistribution of taxpayer monies, forces would be set in motion toward making this a compelling subject that neither the lawmakers, nor the candidates, nor the media could ignore. The unusual credibility of this convergence would likely make this effort quite successful.

Justice O'Connor and Convergence

One of my favorite examples of convergence begins with the continual passion (going for twenty-one years) on behalf of legal services for the needy being pursued by Supreme Court justice and Reagan appointee Sandra Day O'Connor. Years ago, the speeches and writings of this widely and highly regarded conservative jurist astonished me. Now that I know more of conservative philosophy and its own respect for due process and rule of law, I am no longer so astonished. But still, her cutting so clearly through the fog of the power structure that many conservatives allow to mar their public image is still an eyebrow raiser.

Here is Justice O'Connor, speaking for herself before the annual meeting of the American Bar Association in 1991:

> While lawyers have much we can be proud of, we also have a great deal to be ashamed of in terms of how we are responding to the needs of people who can't afford to pay for our services. . . . There has probably never been a wider gulf between the need for legal services and the availability of legal services. . . . Every day, all over the country, people lose their homes or apartments when the law says they should keep them, and people can't feed their children when the law says they should be able to feed them. People don't know the rights they have; even if they know the rights they have, they don't know how to enforce them. And it all has one cause—many people desperately need legal services, but can't afford to pay.[5]

She said that she found that "nearly one quarter of all poor people each year have a civil legal problem deserving a lawyer's attention. But publicly funded attorneys can handle only twelve percent of the load. According to the ABA, eighty percent of poor people's civil legal needs go unmet."[6] That amounts to tens of millions of Americans. Her basic message, grounded in numerous studies, is that when lawyers represent these clients or when they can educate people about how they can invoke the law themselves, far fewer Americans would be evicted from their homes, fewer families would go hungry, fewer people in need would be denied benefits (like Medicaid), and fewer consumers would be gouged.

Justice O'Connor put forth three proposals. First make *mandatory* law school clinical programs to provide legal services for the poor under the supervision of professors.

Second, educate the potential clients themselves. "Often," O'Connor said, "knowing where to go, who to talk to, and which documents to bring will enable someone to solve their problem without the assistance of an attorney." She added, "But our legislation has outpaced our education. . . . This is the kind of project local bar associations are well-placed to organize."[7]

Third, she strongly urged that "a significant percentage of the more than 750,000 practicing lawyers [now more than a million] take on *pro bono* work as a regular part of their practice."[8]

The Justice found the absence of legal services to be shocking, telling her audience of attorneys that "the legal needs of poor people involve the most basic necessities of life, needs like food and shelter." Legal services are even more needed at the present time, with more poor families and more homeowners in the midst of foreclosures.

Progressive jurists and lawyers have long stressed the need for free legal services for the deprived. That is why public defender groups were established early in the twentieth century, and in the sixties the federal Legal Services Corporation was created. It now retains four thousand attorneys to serve the poor. These legal service initiatives were distinctly liberal creations, while later gaining the support, for example, of the American Bar Association as a result of the persuasiveness of Edgar and Jean Cahn, then young progressive graduates of Yale Law School, who drafted the original legislation.

So when conservative Justice O'Connor encouraged a movement to greatly expand pro bono legal services, an opportunity for convergence sprang forth, which could be especially nourished after her retirement from the Supreme Court in 2006. She was freer to advocate this cause more persistently.

A national organization is needed to activate the bar associations, to educate potential clients, and to get more of the 203 law schools in the country to require a place in the curriculum for pro bono legal services.

When Justice William Brennan retired, his scores of law clerks, turned successful lawyers, established the influential Brennan Center at New York University Law School, now with a multimillion-dollar annual budget. Justice O'Connor has a sizeable group of former clerks and supporters in conservative circles around the country who believe in the supremacy of civic values over parochial economic gain in this important area and who could start an O'Connor Center.

Certainly, Justice O'Connor maintains her keen sense of justice. In 2010, she politely chided the majority of the Supreme Court justices in their 5–4 decision known as the *Citizens United* case, with these words: "The Court has created an unwelcome new path for wealthy interests to exert influence on judicial elections."[9]

Foundations or enlightened super-wealthy Americans, whether lawyers or not, able to overcome the obstacles I have outlined in this chapter that discourage coalitions can make possible a new breakthrough in convergence—one grounded solidly in conservative and liberal principles—by recognizing the critical role of the rule of law irrespective of the ability to pay. Given the modest willpower of Justice O'Connor's law clerks and admirers, such a needed institution in short order can become a reality for the long run.

7

Who Owns America?
A Light from the 1930s Illuminates Now

The Robust Conservative Vision of the Thirties

Recovering lost knowledge of our history's justice-sensitive forebears both informs our judgment and motivates further our determination to shape the future.

There was a time in the Depression of the 1930s when conservative thought sprang from the dire concrete reality of that terrible
era, not from abstractions. They did not use the word "conservative" very often, preferring to call themselves "decentralists" or
"agrarians." Eclectic in background they were: columnists, poets,
historians, literary figures, economists, theologians, and civic advocates. In 1936, Herbert Agar, a prominent author, foreign correspondent, and columnist for the *Louisville Courier-Journal* and
Alan Tate, poet and social commentator, brought a selection of
their writings together in a now nearly forgotten book: *Who Owns
America? A New Declaration of Independence.*[1]

In his 1999 foreword to the reissued edition, historian Edward S.
Shapiro called *Who Owns America?* "one of the most significant conservative books published in the United States during the 1930s"

for its "message of demographic, political, and economic decentralization and the widespread ownership of property" in opposition "to the growth of corporate farming, the decay of the small town, and the expansion of centralized political and economic authority."[2]

It is not easy today to convey the intense belief of many activists and intellectuals in the thirties concerning the necessity and inevitability of radical change. Among the best known are the different advocacies that swirled around Roosevelt's liberal New Deal years. They ranged from calls for a strong federal government, with centralizing economic planning, to the ideas of Norman Thomas, the Socialist Party's frequent presidential candidate, who was pushing FDR toward government health insurance, unemployment compensation, Social Security, and labor union rights. Then there were the "spread the wealth" movements of popular figures like Senator Huey Long and radio personalities like Father Coughlin and, in contrast, the Wall Streeters' own challenge: the attempt to save capitalism from President Roosevelt, whom they called a "traitor to his class."

In this mix, there was espoused a political economy for grassroots America that neither Wall Street nor the socialists nor the New Dealers would find acceptable. It came largely out of the agrarian South, casting a baleful eye on both Wall Street and Washington, DC. To these decentralists, the concentrated power of bigness would produce its plutocratic injustices whether regulated through the centralization of political authority in Washington or left to its own monopolistic and cyclical failures. They were quite aware of both the corporate state fast maturing in Italy and Nazi Germany and the Marxists in the Soviet Union constructing another form of concentrated power with an ideology favoring centralized bigness in the state economy. They warned that either approach would produce as an end product unrestrained plutocracy and oligarchy.

Nor did they believe that a federal government with sufficient political authority to modestly tame the plutocracy and what they called "monopoly capitalism" could work, because its struggle would end either in surrender or with the replacing of one set of autocrats with another. As Shapiro wrote in the foreword, "while the plutocrats wanted to shift control over property to themselves, the Marxists wanted to shift this control to government bureaucrats. Liberty would be sacrificed in either case. Only the restoration of the widespread ownership of property, Tate said, could 'create a decent society in terms of American history.'"[3]

Although the decentralists were dismissed by their critics as being impractical, as fighting against the inevitable wave of ever-larger industrial and financial companies empowered by modern technology, their views have a remarkable contemporary resonance given today's globalized gigantism, absentee control, and intricate corporate statism, which are undermining both economies and workers. They started with the effects of concentrated corporate power and its decades-long dispossession of farmers and small business. They rejected abstract theories by focusing instead on such intensifying trends as the separation of ownership from control; the real economy of production in contrast to the manipulative paper economy of finance; and the growth of "wage slavery," farm tenancy, and corporate farming. One can only imagine what they would say today!

Year after year, Agar and his colleagues rejected pyramids of power, saying that the country could have "a majority of small proprietors, with no all-powerful plutocracy at the top and no large proletarian class at the bottom."[4] The decentralists were among the earliest critics of the notion that large industry was inherently more efficient, noting that economies of scale frequently could be met by smaller factories, ones with fewer external costs that would offer fewer abuses to a democratic polity. They revolted against "high finance" at a time of multitiered holding companies, especially in the electrical and other utility industries.

David Cushman Coyle, a prolific economist, put it this way in "The Fallacy of Mass Production": "In a capitalist system, mass

production is usually a mere camouflage for high-finance manip-
ulation of business, to the detriment of the commonwealth and
the impoverishment of the nation."[5] This is why these thinkers insisted on the proximity of direct ownership, in contrast to remote
stock ownership, and, as a result, favored individual proprietorship
and producer and consumer cooperatives. In cases in which large-
scale efficiencies require large-scale operations, they should be run
as "public services." At this time the rural electric cooperatives
were being established for farmers by the US government's Rural
Electrification Administration.

In their arguments they often referred to American history, including the Jeffersonian traditions of smallness and ownership and
the farmers' bitter experience with the large railroads and banks of
the late nineteenth century, which spawned a populist revolt from
east Texas far and wide—to the north, east, and west. They took
repeated note that the farmers' powers—political and economic—
once awakened had their roots in the ownership of their land.

One of their favorite observations of Adam Smith distinguished
between individual capitalism and corporate capitalism. Smith
wrote, "People of the same trade seldom meet together, even for
merriment or diversion, but the conversation ends in a conspiracy
against the public or in some contrivance to raise prices."[6] Wars,
the thirties conservative group believed, only result in the government's creation or support of ever-larger "postwar combines." The
Catholic priest and author John C. Rawe put it this way:

> Corporate mergers and all devices of economic and legal control,
> usurious interest with wholesale foreclosure, unsound manipulation
> of the nation's volume of money by banker, broker, and politician—
> all these have made of us a nation of dispossessed people. . . .
>
>   And it is absolutely irrelevant to learn from government and
> corporation statistics that the total wealth of the nation is much
> greater today than ever before.[7]

Rawe fought not only for *earned distributional justice* but also for the replacement of the "joint-stock agricultural companies," which he wanted outlawed in favor of "cooperative organization." Banks would be superseded by "cooperative credit" institutions owned by the farmers and already spreading in Nebraska and Iowa. He would only concede a role for the federal government's extension service to help farmers learn how "to function cooperatively, in the intricate business of marketing their products," and how to operate their farms efficiently.

Rawe and other agrarians were not easily fooled. They knew that only a *shift of power* from the plutocrats to the farmers and others would produce the desired social justice. "No State or Federal regulation," wrote Rawe, "is ever adequately enforced to protect private individual owners in any field of commercial production. The immense power of the incorporated monopoly always has its ways of circumventing legislative programs."[8] Sound familiar?

The Decentralizers' Conservative Thought Closer to the Ground Than That of Today's Rightists

The "decentralists" had a concrete awareness of the ways and means of corporate power, that was way ahead of many of today's conservative thinkers, who believe that the marketplace will suffice to check this ever-boiling force of business power from damaging overreach. Many contemporary conservatives exhibit such a focus on government and keeping it at arm's length that they have neglected to rigorously propose an alternative locus of power, one that would take up many functions of government and restrict what they contemptuously call "crony capitalism." Part of the reason for this contrast between thinkers of the Depression years and the ones we have now is that the earlier conservative writers were close to the dirt-level poverty, land dispossession, foreclosures, and the overturning by Big Business of a historic way of rural life, which empirically grounded their diagnoses and reforms. There were no screens to look at daily in their abstract workplaces and households to distract them from grim reality.

What was also remarkable about this intellectual ferment was the fundamental range and depth of their pursuits. They refused to grant legitimacy to corporate claims of having the same constitutional rights given to people. They knew how little accountability their state charters asked of business entities. Vanderbilt University professor Lyle H. Lanier in his essay, "Big Business in the Property State," launched a critique by citing Chief Justice John Marshall's famous words that each corporation is an "artificial being, invisible, intangible, and existing only in the contemplation of the law." Lanier wondered how "in this land of rugged individualism two hundred corporations control more than fifty percent of the nation's industrial assets." He continued:

> Conceived in that constitutional Garden of Eden whose walls are the Fifth and the Fourteenth Amendments, and nurtured by the friendly decisions of a judiciary saturated with ex-lawyers of corporations, these economic giants have become the instruments of an economic fascism which threatens the essential democratic institutions of America. . . . Ironically enough, the most vociferous defenders of free competitive enterprise are the big industrialists and their lawyers, whose illicit appeal to the sentiments properly attaching to the institution of private ownership of real property has served to camouflage the development of an alien economic system.[9]

"In these matters," he continued, "America is confronted with a condition, not a theory. It is obvious that the peculiar disassociation of ownership from control of property, which characterizes the corporation, and the reduction of a progressively increasing number of real property owners to the status of wage-earners, create conditions not contemplated by the founders of the American Republic."[10]

Today, the financial, industrial, and commercial stock corporations care far less about ownership than about control. Ironically, the greatest wealth in this country is still owned by the people but controlled by the corporations under the approving aegis of the federal and state governments. These assets are owned under individual claims, in the case of pensions and stocks, and as a commons in the case of the public lands, the public airwaves, and the varieties of government research, development, and other public assets. All are peoples' assets controlled and taken by corporate power for profit.

To the agrarians and decentralists of eighty years ago, the distinction was democratically unsustainable. As Alan Tate wrote: "Ownership and control are property. Ownership without control is slavery because control without ownership is tyranny. . . . Corporate property has reached gigantic dimensions under protections of certain legal fictions: when the law made the abstract corporation a person, gifted with the privilege of real persons but with few of the responsibilities, it established a fiction that has gradually undermined the traditional safeguards, the truly functional property rights, embodied in the older common law."[11]

These writers' clarity on matters of the traditional queries by political thinkers—the who, what, when and how of power—made them quick to debunk distracting ploys, like the growth of the GDP, as justifying the status quo of corporatism. They went right to the distribution question, as did, by the way, Henry Ford in 1914, when he doubled the daily wages of his workers to $5 so that there were more buyers for his cars.

Lyle Lanier liked to quote the famous and very well-paid president of General Motors, Alfred P. Sloan, who, in Sloan's words, advocated a "broader distribution of income in order that a condition of abundance rather than of scarcity might prevail."[12] Too bad that Walmart executives did not adopt their policies to follow that basic curve of American economic progress: namely, that higher wages lead to more basic consumption and economic expansion. Walmart has been the leader in reversing this years-long curve with a low-wage policy it has mercilessly inflicted on its workers and its domestic suppliers, which it has forced to meet the "China price" or to relocate production to China.

Lanier was unrelenting but still in the mainstream of agrarian conservative framing. He favored a tax on corporations that advantaged any company "which maintained as low a ratio as possible between volume of business on the one hand and net earnings and salaries on the other."

Because he viewed government regulation of wages to be impractical, he favored the "only feasible resource": collective bargaining by labor. His rationale would be fresh and clear-eyed today: "In the typical big corporations the management represents the collective interests of great numbers of 'owners,' and possesses enormous power by virtue of that fact. The collective interests of the workers in the plant should be represented by an organized leadership, which would aim to secure for each individual an equitable return from the productive activity of the concern." He recognized that both corporations and labor unions may "frequently be guilty of racketeering practices" (note the evenhandedness rarely found in today's self-described conservatives), but "vertical industrial unions will be economically desirable and socially necessary in big mass-production enterprises."[13] Lanier shared the wide belief that the "labor problem" could be diminished by decentralization and widespread small ownership.

Not until later in the 1990s did the decentralists' core focus on corporate power and personhood begin to be discussed even in liberal/progressive circles. Yet, back in the 1930s, Lanier had put the central issue concisely: "The farce of treating these giant corporations as individuals with the rights and privileges of individual American citizens should be discontinued. Constitutional amendment is the only recourse."[14]

Meanwhile, the agrarians were pleased to note that the populist wave coursing through the Midwest farm belt was moving to pass state laws prohibiting charters from being awarded to any corporation engaging in agriculture. Kansas led the way in this direction, even applying "capital punishment" in 1932 by revoking the charter of the Wheat Farming Corporation—a Moloch acquiring tens of thousands of acres and removing from them the houses and barns along with the hard-pressed family farmers. What the decentralists were pushing for was the supremacy of individual property rights that "secure life, liberty and the pursuit of happiness," over the property rights of incorporated entities possessing a "legal-social structure of privilege and concentration completely alien" to the agrarians' notions of a democratic society. In this regard, they drew their public's attention to the early corporate chartering laws, administered by state legislatures in the early 1800s with "the greatest caution and limitation," reflecting the charterers' view of the supremacy of property "in the hands of private individuals."[15] Rapid industrialism and the increase in the power of financial institutions led to the changing of these laws and the revising of some state constitutions to authorize more automatic chartering by state agencies, leading the agrarians to lament the lost opportunity, for they had been pressing for the creation of chartered cooperatives that would do the same work of amassing capital and other services without their displaying the distorting greed and concentrated power of corporations. Pragmatic to the end, short of that cooperative vision, they expounded numerous reforms to make both corporate executives and corporations more responsible for their "workmen" and "their modified ownership."

However they enumerated the "collectivist" power of the giant corporations and their governmental servants, the agrarian decentralists were not in awe of such power. In 1933, under emergency conditions of their own making, the "great lords of banking, who are said to hold us in the palms of their hands, were as gentle as the hearth-side of altered cats," wrote Herbert Agar, adding that "they asked the government please to save them, please to protect them from the alleged anger of the public."[16]

If the American people, Agar believed, "ever decide they want something, they will not be headed off by anyone so readily frightened as our robber rabbits. . . . The important question from our point of view is not whether we can overcome the opposition of Big Business, but whether we can convince the plain man in America that our program is what he wants."[17] Here Agar struck the bell of democracy that has tolled for the people everywhere.

The real danger, the decentralists believed, in the awakening of the people, was the demagogues (they would name Senator Huey Long or Dr. Townsend) preying on the lower middle classes by promising them the moon and offering simple solutions. If the demagogue comes to power, knowing he has no easy solution, he will turn, in Agar's indictment, to

> the Lords and Masters . . . and make a deal. The demagogue stays in office and keeps the people quiet. The Lords and Masters stay in power and run the economic system just the way they always wanted to run it. The corporate state is monopoly-capitalism made safe. One of the first steps is to destroy all labor unions. Then the plain man is fobbed off with subsistence wages, patriotism, and a uniform. If he is still restive, it is not hard to fling him some racial minority on whom to work off his spleen. The Jews do very nicely. In America the Negroes might also serve.[18]

Presently, in ways the decentralists could never have conceived or believed possible, the "Lords and Masters" did not need street revolts led by fascistic demagogues, who ask the Lords to join together in a mutually beneficial collaboration. During the collapse of 2008–2009, the "Lords and Masters" simply sent their A-Team from Wall Street to save themselves *by becoming the government,* led by former Goldman Sachs chief Henry Paulson, the secretary of the Treasury. Referring to the one-way, unlawful rescue extravaganzas under George W. Bush, Mr. Paulson stunningly admitted to the *Washington Post* that he "didn't have the authorities" but someone had to do it.[19]

It is remarkable how deeply and concretely these earlier defenders of prudence and tradition kept abreast of the new perils of the corporate supremacists. The Depression years of the thirties made many thinkers and doers get down to fundamentals, whether they were in the social sciences, humanities, or the arts or organizing actions in communities. They thought more boldly, spoke out more candidly, confronted the realities of power, and, even when they were dealing with abstract principles, sought to ground their thoughts in the real world where people live and work. The agrarian decentralists did not indulge in pussy-footing or the other verbal cadences of avoidance when it came to fingering the perverse structures of the political economy and naming how they were responsible for exploitation, greed, repression, and dispossession. But then they did not have to go to their offices every day to work in rarified, screen-filled environments, being well-paid by grants from economic interests, vested ideologues, or foundations. The decentralists and agrarians had relatives and friends in serious states of impoverishment and insecurity, and if they did not, they saw these avoidable, wretched conditions all around them. It was hard to live a lie. Unemployment was as high as 25 percent to 45 percent, depending on the area.

Even with Their Limitations, the Agrarians Had a Keen Eye for the Dangers of the Corporations

They had their limitations when it came to directly discussing race. African-Americans were not given much attention, other than to be included in their denunciations of all sharecropping. Property ownership begat freedom, but also tenancy and other forms of what they considered servitude.

Women were also not given specific attention in their rendition of "life, liberty and the pursuit of happiness." They wrote about "the people" generally. But one chapter in *Who Owns America?*, titled "The Emancipated Woman," by Vassar College professor Mary Shattuck Fisher, minced no words right from the beginning: "To call the modern American woman free is as false as to call modern America a democracy, and for the same reasons. She is not living in a world whose values are based on a sense of the worth of human beings, or one characterized by equality before the law and equality of opportunity. That is why she is not free, however 'emancipated.' It is also the reason why America is not a democracy."[20] Professor Fisher was not at all wowed by the increasing number of women in the workplace, seeing them as entering the same rat race that men are gripped by, though they were coming in at a lower wage rate and also had to shoulder the "double burden of maternity and employment." These women, she added, "do not suspect that the present development of productive forces could provide the groundwork for more security and more happiness if only it were operated on democratic principles. They are too bitterly deprived, too much concerned with keeping alive to care to understand such matters."[21]

She was one tough feminist, excoriating her gender, post-1920 (the year when the Nineteenth Amendment gave women the right to vote), for failing to use their vote effectively, because "like their male relatives, [they] are ignorant, bewildered, helpless or indifferent in the face of concealed minorities, of machine government and political corruption. . . . Women have not even attempted to turn things upside down, as it was once feared they would do. . . . They are coming to feel that it is of no use to vote."[22]

Troy J. Cauley, an economist and author of the acclaimed book *Agrarianism: A Program for Farmers* (1935), questioned the program advanced by the philosophy called "technocracy," which foresaw a future in which there would be a redistribution of property from the few to the many, or even abundance with less work for all, powered by increasing automation. None of those schemes, he asserted, offered any "method for redistributing property among the people." He went even deeper: "If there is to be a stable and permanent foundation for a redistribution of income, the foundation must be a general diffusion of property ownership, that is, a general diffusion of the control of the sources of income."[23]

Cauley wanted to achieve this diffusion through a democracy, which he believed had a greater chance of rapid advancement than a "country controlled by a dictatorship either communist or fascist," which would not achieve or want such decentralization in any event. Though like most reformers, who shun the path of dictating the exact steps to be taken to effect a change, he and his colleagues offered no specific steps to get to the goal of distributing property, which today may be called a "variety of capital assets," among the people. Further, he insisted on the need for a society that enhances spiritual and "other non-material wants." He knew where it must all start. "For in the last analysis, community life and family life have much the same essential bases."[24]

The decentralists were not alone in not knowing how to get to their secure and free society—an unanswered question that still haunts today's advocates of just change. Nevertheless, these writers and scholars, coming off the destitutions of the most prolonged economic collapse and massive unemployment in American history, known as the Great Depression, have much to teach us during these times known, so far, as the Great Recession. Their writings shame the thinness of the conservative/liberal appraisals of the contemporary contours of power and control. They were much freer of taboos. They liberated themselves from the latent self-censorship that in our era has for years precluded fresh thought about even modest power-shifting possibilities and civic motivations. (These include simple mechanisms, such as checkoffs and organized refunds for new consumer and labor advocacy groups, which could work prudently and increasingly to shift some balance of power away from the plutocrats and oligarchs who desiccate our national pretensions.) They also had a clear-eyed focus on the grip of the giant corporations over our political economy, whose antagonism to our sense of individual and community freedom and fair access to justice (courts and agencies) is so palpable today. Most outstanding was their persistent questioning as to why the artificial entity that is the "joint-stock company" should have ever achieved equality with human beings under our Constitution, a document that starts with "We the people" and never mentions the words "corporation" or "company" or proclaims "We the corporation."

Now and Then:
How Much Less Clear-Eyed
Today's Reformers Are

Ironically, compared to their time, there is now an overwhelmingly larger production of printed, documentary, and Internet video materials conveying what abuses of all kinds are doing to people and their institutions. There are more freely accessible, theoretical, empirical, statistical, and mathematical materials purporting to demonstrate one economic, political, or philosophical position after another, many contesting the current arrangements of power. Why aren't they stimulating change?

This generation is growing up in the greatest golden age of exposés and muckraking in American history. Yet these revelations and declarations seem to have less and less follow-up, less effect on legislators, major party candidates, regulators, prosecutors, and educators. Some attribute this lack of action to overload—"injustice fatigue"—but that's an immature excuse. A better explanation is that the misuses of power and the rampant commercialization and bureaucratization of almost everything *have weakened our democratic institutions*. They have eroded our civic sense of community and marginalized our little-reported, modest countervailing powers, such as any activity by trade unions and family farms' groups. While information is the currency of democracy, there has been little carry-forward of this plethora of information to mobilization. To put it in historical context, I do not believe that the consumer, environmental, and labor reforms of the sixties and early seventies could have happened in this decade. Even worse, the struggle now is to thwart rollbacks and repeals of the accomplishments of that period of popular progress.

Since those days of progress, there has been a shift in the type of political representatives in Washington, who are now nearly all dialing ferociously for the same commercial dollars; there has been the gerrymandering out of even two-party competition, the placement of many business executives in government posts, and the strengthening of mass corporate lobbying, from AstroTurf to Capitol Hill. All these factors have made some contributions to this decline. It matters little that Congress is now live on C-SPAN everywhere, given these shifts. Also among changes not to be discounted is the business leverage, which comes from the multinational corporations' ability to move jobs and operations abroad and the use of that mobility to sustain their power-grabbing ways in the United States.

There is something else to ponder. Reformist agendas document the need for change and make recommendations that touch on the described or depicted symptoms. Except for the work of a few people like Professor Lawrence Goodwyn (*The Populist Moment*) or Richard Grossman and Ward Morehouse, who reintroduced the forgotten corporate history of chartering, personhood, and the actions of the populists, the decentralists, and agrarians, today's avalanche of materials does not reach the core of the recidivist power structures. Moreover, as has already been examined, the two-party duopoly (or tyranny) has successfully excluded third parties, which have tried to challenge the two major parties over these issues. Through a growing variety of ballot access obstacles' harassment of petitioners; baseless, exhausting litigation during election years; "top two" primary laws; and exclusion from televised debates—all propped up by a winner-take-all system cum the atavistic electoral college—the electoral doors are closed to basic challenges.

Updating the Vision of the Thirties Decentralizers

Reading through *Who Owns America?* and related outcries from the thirties provides an enlightening contrast to what one finds in the statist assertions expressed by the various spokespeople for "isms." And such a reading should stimulate the LC toward convergence even more.

Merely updating these "conservative" constructs on property, ownership, control, corporate privileges and immunities, and government regulation can help to clarify deliberations between Lib-Cons. The expansion of property owned but not controlled by the people has moved into the trillions of dollars through such means as worker pensions, enormous government transfers of taxpayer-funded research and development (e.g., intellectual property), the corporatization of public works and, of course, the public lands, public airwaves, and Internet. Yet, year after year, political campaigns by the two parties totally ignore this critical invasion of the commons.

Corporate privileges and immunities have also rapidly expanded in degree and in kind. Corporate welfare is immensely more varied, larger, and bipartisan. Corporations have devised, with their corporate lawyers, significant escapes from accountability. They have moved from having limited liability for their shareholders to ever more limited liability for the corporate entity itself, and now onto practical immunities for the top executives and directors. The Price Anderson Act limits the liability and insurability of atomic power plant utilities to a fraction of the potential damages accidents at these facilities would entail by shifting the financial burdens of disasters to the state (i.e., to taxpayers). Federal loan guarantees insure corporate capitalism. The awarding of defense industry corporation contracts carries special sovereign immunities with them. And, equally insidious, the shredding of tort law and the constant employment of one-sided, fine-print vendor contracts are collapsing two major pillars of our law while narrowing popular access to remedial justice and deterrence.

These seismic transitions proliferate outside public consciousness, business and law school educations, and, of course, the political electoral arenas. The immunity wave that has led to the replacement of responsibility and accountability is almost never discussed—a veritable, gigantic, quiet taboo. A corollary shield from criminal law for corporate malefactors is created by the fact that tiny government enforcement budgets have led routinely to plea bargains that permit modest settlements but no admission of guilt. No-fault government, no-fault giant corporations, and no-choice elections have become institutionalized against basic challenges by the people.

Meanwhile, government regulations have also been overtaken by the phenomenon of "regulatory capture," as studiously pointed out by conservative economist George Stigler decades ago, though now put through with far greater sophistication and legislative assistance in favor of the regulatees and their insistent lobbyists and law firms. Making sure federal cops on the corporate crime beats have stripped budgets is another systemic strategy used by companies these days to keep their activities from scrutiny. The corporate crime wave, with its costs and corruption of government, reaches new intensities every decade, as there is more to take from the public purse.

The Financial Meltdown as a Fine Illustration of Corporate Impunity

That there is a broader immunity breakthrough was pointed out in August 2012 in the *New York Times* by writer Jesse Eisinger. Even when the protagonists of deregulation, in this case the financial firms that lobbied to repeal Glass-Steagall and led to wild financial risk taking and disasters for our economy during Wall Street's self-inflicted collapse, and even when its principal promoters, such as Sanford Weill, the grand consolidator of Citigroup, regret what they did, thereby (to a degree) admitting their responsibility for the disasters, there are no authoritative calls for significant legal, occupational, or social sanctions against them.

Far from it. Here is Jesse Eisinger's lament, titled "As Banking Titans Reflect on Errors, Few Pay Any Price":

> As every frustrated American knows, no major banking executive has gone to prison or has been fined any significant amount in the aftermath of the financial crisis.
>
> But what's astonishing is that Wall Street bankers seem not to have paid any social cost either. They sit on corporate and nonprofit boards and attend functions and galas. They remain top Wall Street executives, or even serve as regulators. The nation's prominent op-ed pages, talk shows and conferences seek their opinions. If you are rich, you must be intelligent. Your views must be worthwhile, never mind the track record.
>
> The embrace of Mr. Weill sets a new standard for reputation rehabilitation. . . . Mr. Weill's only unambiguous success was to make himself enormously rich.

After recounting the serial collapse of the Citigroup Worldwide empire and its numerous scandals and violations of the law during the past generation, Mr. Eisinger asks, "What's a guy gotta do around here to lose a little credibility?"[25]

Former secretary of the Treasury under Clinton and shortly thereafter co-chair of Citigroup, Robert Rubin should be asking the same question. He profited immensely from the Citigroup mess—the company lost billions in the 2008 meltdown and had to be rescued by the government afterward—and was proven wrong, but he still rides high, appearing right after the crisis in November 2008 in a photograph with a select group of invited advisors, next to the just-elected President Barack Obama. It was Rubin who lobbied from his government post in 1999 to repeal Glass-Steagall. A year later he opposed a bill to regulate burgeoning trading in riskier derivatives, one of the newly allowed results of the repeal whereby investment banking and commercial banking could be mixed, a process that erupted and eventually led to the spectacular speculative bust. It was Rubin, knowing the repeal of Glass-Steagall was imminent, who resigned his Treasury post and rushed to make $40 million in a few weeks, advising Citigroup in the fall of 1999. It was co-chair Rubin whose strategies helped steer the ship of Citigroup onto the rocks while he himself was still making big money.

He has not yet recanted from the gigantic folly of his concoctions. He is still sought after for interviews, except about his role as an escape artist, and invited to give advice to potentates and politicians. Rubin experiences no shunning and is on the social circuit in New York and Washington, DC. Nassim Taleb, author of the super-bestseller *The Black Swan* and financial scholar, says of Mr. Rubin that "nobody on this planet represents more vividly the scam of the banking industry."[26] As Jesse Eisinger said: "What's a guy gotta do around here to lose a little credibility?"

The Good Old Days When Corporate Criminals Actually Went to Jail

These two cases, and the many like them, are telltale signs of the rapid decay of any kinds of restraining or punitive sanctions being given to those who perpetrate serious corporate misdeeds, a decay made more visible when today's situation is compared to what happened in the previous bank collapse of the savings and loans twenty years ago, when hundreds of bank officials went to jail.

One other problem is that the deep and reckless pushing further of the frontiers of immunities for the corporate power structure does not occur within any recognized legal or ethical frameworks around which public dialogue and electoral contests can engage. This is in marked contrast to what was available at the time of the decentralists, whose moral vision of the good life and startling ability to go beyond economics and doctrinaire ideologies put such corporate skullduggery in perspective. This fully justifies our giving their views a closer look in the historical contexts of their and our time. Certainly their view of localism, small business, and cooperative-style ownership is still resonant and is being put into practice by the current spread of community economies, as noted earlier, facilitating wide new possibilities by harnessing locally many recalled and modern technologies. These modes of life re-ject the "servility, and regimentation, [and] degradation of human values," in the words of Professor Shapiro's foreword to *Who Owns America?*.[27] But they need the expanded public consciousness that would give them greater diffusion.

To those who would say that it's always been that way, corpo-rate criminals have always gotten away with it, the historical reply is "not quite." Many high Wall Street operators went to jail after the October 1929 stock market crash. The president of the New York Stock Exchange, patrician Richard Whitney, went up the Hudson to Sing Sing Prison; photographs of him in handcuffs were printed on page 1 of the country's newspapers. President Frank-lin D. Roosevelt denounced these reckless bankers and speculators as the "enemies of peace," and he named strong regulators to the new federal law enforcement agencies.

Yet now the latest gang of Wall Street miscreants walk free. I have seen neither studies nor any explanation that would suggest how to reverse the frustrated public acceptance of this fact, other than putting pressure on Congress and the White House. Not-withstanding C-SPAN, twenty-four-hour cable news, finger-tip

Internet, and access to the blogs and websites of dissidents and rebels, the anomie of the populace taken together just deepens. From somewhere we need a spark to action leading to a surge of civic determination to activate our constitutional authorities and assert our sovereignty. The people's sense of injustice is widespread enough to warrant some optimism.

The Forward Legacy of *Who Owns America?*

Not surprisingly, when *Who Owns America?* came out on April 28, 1936—a presidential election year—it did not have much influence on contemporary politics. All over, schools of thought, political practices, and public earnestness were concentrating on *relief*, not basic *reform*. But concrete, principled ideas matter, and they can lie fallow for years before the times afford the proper soil for their seeds to sprout.

There were reviews of *Who Owns America?* in major newspapers and magazines that pointed to the decentralists and agrarians as impractical utopians, out of touch with the inevitability of Big Business, big industry, and these entities' own possible discipliner—the federal government. After all, at the time the people had a president whose fireside radio speeches satisfied many Americans who needed a perceived champion against concentrated power. An FDR sample: "I should like to have it said of my Administration that in it the forces of selfishness and of lust for power met their match. I should like to have it said of my second Administration that in it these forces met their master."[28] But Professor Shapiro does quote one notable commentary by the publisher of the *American Review*, Seward Collins, who called *Who Owns America?* "the most significant book produced by the depression. It contains more sanity and penetration, more sense of American realities and American history, more grasp of economic fundamentals, more enlightened moral passion, more insight into what is happening and . . . into what will happen than the whole monstrous spate of depression books put together."[29]

Today we live in a polity possessed of shrunken perspectives, where elective offices are political sinecures, with the occupants serving corporate bosses. Almost all the politicians are for sale— with few enough successful exceptions to point to as the preferable, contrasting alternative of politicians actually concerned with the good of the people. The 24/7 distractions of Internet and video inundations have given birth to a new generation of aliterates with alarmingly shortened attention spans.[30] Worse by the year, historically deprived youngsters are split off from their own communities and neighborhoods, with which they scarcely interact, preferring to be glued to, even addicted to, watching screens hour after hour, sitting entranced while clutching their iPhones in their hands. Yet, even in this state, some young people are still reading. Let's hope they get their hands on books such as the one I have scrutinized in this chapter.

Who Owns America? is the question for our times, immersed in expanding urgencies that cry out, "Take heed, take heed, or pay the price!"

8

Common Ground for
Common and Uncommon Causes,
Found in the Thoughts of Much-Cited
but Little-Read Conservative Icons

The previous chapter, as well as my earlier remarks on the unorthodox thoughts of various much-cited but seldom-read icons of conservatism, has shown us that by shattering images and avoiding cherry-picking, progressive readers of conservative/libertarian literature will come to the conclusion that, program by program, there is plenty of room for LCs to converge and work together on system-altering actions.

One by one, the titans of the Right demonstrate that their principles are not frozen against the tides of realities and their own human values. A few more remarks on the flexibility of these icons might be apropos here. Friedrich Hayek wrote that the state should assure a base income to all the poor under its jurisdiction. The Austrian economist also declared the need for "a legal system designed both to preserve competition and to make it operate as beneficially as possible."[1] Carl T. Bogus, a biographer of William F. Buckley Jr., wrote that Hayek "advocated regulatory mechanisms to prevent fraud, deception, and monopolies, and said there was a strong case for government providing 'some minimum of food, shelter, and clothing, sufficient to preserve health and capacity to work,' and organizing a comprehensive system of social insurance for sickness and accidents. Nevertheless, the principal theme of his work tied together freedom, democracy, and capitalism."[2] All were tied together to oppose socialism. Adam Smith noted "the interest of the producer ought to be attended to only so far as it may be necessary for promoting that of the consumer."[3]

That is a lot of common ground shared with progressives, visible once the selective references to Hayek's work by today's Paul Ryans are cast aside. As economist Peter Boettke of George Mason University and editor of the *Review of Austrian Economics* has said: "What Hayek has become, to a lot of people, is an iconic figure representing something that he didn't believe at all."[4] What Hayek intensely opposed was government planning of the economy and its inherent complexity, corporate subsidies, chronic deficit spending, government housing programs, and any state initiative that is not applicable to all the citizenry. Illustratively, he opposed Medicare and Medicaid unless they were applicable to all citizens.

Neither Russell Kirk, who referred to the grasping super-rich as "a host of squalid oligarchs,"[5] nor Henry Calvert Simons, one of the founders of the conservative Chicago School of Economics, and a major mentor of Milton Friedman, had any illusions about who was running the economy.

Here are Simons's prescriptions, written in the Depression (1934) as an essay, "A Positive Program for Laissez Faire," to bring private enterprise to its potential:

> Eliminate all forms of monopolistic market power, to include the breakup of large oligopolistic corporations and application of anti-trust laws to labor unions. A Federal incorporation law could be used to limit corporation size and where technology required giant firms for reasons of low cost production, the Federal govern-

ment should own and operate them. . . . Promote economic stability by reform of the monetary system and establishment of stable rules for monetary policy. . . . Reform the tax system and promote equity through income tax. . . . Abolish all tariffs. . . . Limit waste by restricting advertising and other wasteful merchandising practices.[6]

Compare the economic stands of Simons with those of his cruel corporatist successors at the Chicago school, who would not consider moving against even the financial conglomerates that brought down the economy in 2008–2009 and that now, in 2014, are even more concentrated and "too big to fail."

Milton Friedman and Richard Nixon both supported a "negative income tax" that led to an earned income tax credit for poor people with children. In a debate I had with Milton Friedman, he reluctantly admitted that government regulation—and was he ever against just about every government regulation from tariffs to licensing of doctors to car safety—had to be applied to pollution. Even the biggest conservative icon of them all, Adam Smith, was big on public works. Smith also "maintained that a chief goal of taxation should be 'to remedy inequality of riches as much as possible by relieving the poor and burdening the rich.'"[7]

But let's move from thinkers to doers and examine some of the flexibility found in conservative politicians of the past. Senator Robert Taft was the towering Mr. Conservative in Washington after World War II. His father was William Howard Taft, president of the United States and later chief justice of the Supreme Court. As president, William Howard Taft supported the Sixteenth Amendment authorizing the income tax, went after big monopolies with many antitrust prosecutions, and backed regulation of railroad rates. His conservative standard-bearer son was even more surprising. While Senator Taft had been a supporter of Herbert Hoover and opposed Roosevelt's New Deal's "socialistic experiments without paying for them," he was anything but a clenched-jaw ideologue.[8] Remarkably, the Senator favored taxing investment income before taxing income on labor. As Bogus relates: "In the early days of the New Deal, he favored price controls for oil and coal, some forms of debtor relief, and spending $3 billion ('but no more' for public works programs). He supported old-age pensions, increasing payments for the health of mothers and children, and some unemployment insurance under Social Security, but he did not want to extend coverage too far."[9] Believing that the free enterprise system "has certain definite limits," he accorded the state a role in reducing poverty. In Taft's words, the federal government should "put a floor under essential things to give all a minimum standard of living, and all children an opportunity to get a start in life."[10]

Raising the eyebrows, if not ire, of some of his fellow conservatives, Senator Taft voted for FHA loans to home purchasers and for constructing public housing for the poor. After a visit in 1943 to Puerto Rico, where he witnessed grievous poverty, he became a strong champion of federal aid to education. Accused of being socialistic by his hidebound, right-wing peers, Taft showed his pragmatism by retorting: "Education is socialistic anyhow, and has been for 150 years."[11]

Here are some other statements and stances adopted by Taft in a time when they were not conventional positions.

As to racist attitudes, he stated, "I see no reason to think that inequality of intellect or ability is based on racial origin,"[12] and he opposed poll taxes and discrimination against African Americans. In 1942, going against such liberals as FDR and California governor Earl Warren, he was the only lawmaker in Congress to question the internment of Japanese Americans after Pearl Harbor.

The notorious anti-union Taft-Hartley law of 1947 bore his name and active advocacy, though he believed in the workers' right to collective bargaining and to strike. He even blocked President Truman's outrageous but then-popular demand that Congress enact legislation allowing him to draft strikers who he believed jeopardized the national welfare. Taft believed the 1947 law would create a better balance between labor and management. Two years later, he saw the opposite had happened—that the law heavily favored management—and he wanted to amend it accordingly to achieve the hoped-for balance. The unions wanted total repeal, and they ended up with nothing. Sixty-seven years later, Taft-Hartley has stayed unchanged.

On foreign and military policy, he presciently warned against our nation becoming "a garrison state," being imperialistic, and spending too much on military budgets and non–disaster-related foreign aid. He did not believe that the Soviet Union wanted war with the United States or with Western Europe. For this he was labeled an "isolationist."

Compared to his relatively nonbelligerent views against Western European defense involvement, Taft was a hawk in Asia, opposing Communist China, calling for an escalation of the war in Korea, and supporting Chiang Kai-shek and Formosa. Generally, however, he was an exponent of using reason and reality to guide political philosophy, in strong contrast to today's Republican "nattering nabobs of negativism" (using Spiro Agnew's words in a new context), who blockade the Senate and House of Representatives.

It was President Richard Nixon who recognized Communist China, made arms control agreements with the Soviet Union, proposed a national health insurance scheme that was better than Clinton's, wanted a drug policy emphasizing rehabilitation over incarceration, got rid of the gold standard, and, apostasy itself, instituted wage and price controls to restrain inflation. All these and other signed enactments by Nixon of new regulatory agencies outraged William F. Buckley and William A. Rusher of the *National Review*.

This accounting, which has detailed some of the eminently sensible and progressive attitudes of many famed conservatives, both thinkers and politicians, could be extended, but enough has been said to indicate that any progressive who seriously delves into conservative thought will find much common ground, on which can be built LC convergences.

9

What of the Liberals?
And Populist Conservatives?

Liberals' Shibboleths and Weaknesses

What of the liberal/progressive intellectual tradition over the past century or so? That is, after the period when "classical liberalism" became so accepted, even thinkers viewed as conservatives would adhere to its stance on individual and religious freedoms, private property protection, civil rights, curbs on arbitrary government, and the rule of law.

If we go beyond the eighteenth- and nineteenth-century "classical liberalism," in which conservatives also find their roots, we see the Left does not possess the kind of revered champions, delineating norms and guarding its frameworks of thought, as found among conservatives and libertarians. Political economist Jeff Faux, founder of the Economic Policy Institute in Washington, DC, believes that Henry George, Harold Laski, Eugene Debs, and the institutionalists like John R. Commons and Thorstein Veblen, filled the role of liberal sages in their day. But starting with the age of FDR, much of the Left became very practical, eschewing the grand philosophies that could be equated with the persecuted adherents of domestic socialism or communism—a fear of being equated with these "isms" whose characterizations were defined by the prominent accusatory career of Senator Joseph McCarthy. For himself, FDR was content with telling American workers to join unions.

Consumer and later environmental advocates were stiffly empirical, evidence- and exposé-oriented, avoiding more sweeping ideologies. The New Left in the sixties, Faux says, had very little connection with the past, sometimes even ridiculing its elders and the intellectual output from the Great Depression. The New Left was going for a cultural revolution, expanding individual rights and behaviors, eschewing wars with the cry "Hell no, we won't go" or "Make love, not war," while showing little interest in establishing institutions to carry forward. There was, Faux, says "a lack of seriousness in ideas."[1]

Liberals have been mostly programmatic—a mode of operation that connects with reality. Ask them what they espouse, and you'll see. But the energy behind this pragmatic attitude begins to dry up without the nourishment of a larger philosophic or general vision. So it has come to pass that liberals and, to a lesser extent, progressives must own up to their own shibboleths and weaknesses if convergence is to widen beyond the easy areas of agreement.

Over the years, many outspoken liberals/progressives were not as attuned to communist despotism—its end purposes were said to be fairer—as they were to fascist despotism. This began to change with the Soviet invasion of Hungary in 1956 to put down popular resistance to the domestic communist government. Moreover, they turned away from facing up to union leaders' corruption even as they excoriated corporate corruption. They overlooked serious and violent corruption at the top of the United Mine Workers in the last years of the sixties and later in the Teamsters, which joined with trucking companies to force drivers to run unsafe rigs. Some of us criticized repression of the rank-and-file workers by union officials when it came to union governance and worker rights. None of these criticisms, which would have strengthened unions, were received with much enthusiasm by liberal politicians and writers, who, allied with unions on other important issues, felt constrained to look the other way.

Liberals/progressives have also feared that any criticisms of social welfare programs would jeopardize their existence or their needed budgets. So they would overlook the waste and unintended consequences of bureaucratized dispensing agencies. Coming late to this problem set up the Clinton-era mischief called "workfare," administered by the likes of Lockheed Martin and intended to get aid recipients to take jobs for unlivable wages, assuming the cut-loose welfare mothers could get them in the first place. All this emphasis on welfare abuse also distracted politicians from addressing the burgeoning corporate welfare extravaganzas draining far more of the taxpayers' dollars than do poverty welfare payments. Not confronting the hard edges of these poverty programs also allowed the avowed terminators of such programs to daunt or co-opt more reasonable conservatives in the tradition of Senator Robert Taft, conservatives who could have pushed reform efforts that shed the negatives and strengthened the positives of these compassionate programs for the sick, maimed, impoverished, or unlucky people of all ages in our country.

Here is an opportunity for convergence that the extreme right wing would do everything it could to block, especially by relying on the absolutist, often sneering daily media presentations on their radio and cable talk shows, led by mega-millionaires Rush Limbaugh, Sean Hannity, and Michael Savage (themselves being enriched by the corporate welfare of free radio licenses to use the public airwaves). As professor Robert Brent Toplin noted: "The militant right has distorted the meaning of conservatism to the point that . . . much that passes as 'conservative' does not truly represent the principles of intelligent, responsible, and thoughtful conservatism."[2]

A column by the peripatetic reporter Nicholas D. Kristof in the December 9, 2012, edition of the *New York Times* provided a "heartbreaking" example of what can happen when the Left avoids forthright examination of some perverse incentives of poverty programs, which makes these programs sitting ducks for the extreme right while scaring off thoughtful, compassionate conservatives from finding any good in the broader goals of the programs.

Kristof was in Jackson, Kentucky—a poverty-belt area, long classified as afflicted with endemic unemployment. He describes "parents here in Appalachian pulling their children out of literacy classes. Moms and dads fear that if kids learn to read, they are less likely to qualify for a monthly check [of up to $698] for having [a child with] an intellectual disability."[3]

Now suppose an unintimidated convergence climate was in existence forty years ago, when President Richard Nixon, adopting an idea of Milton Friedman advanced by Democrat Daniel P. Moynihan (Nixon's White House advisor), called for a "minimum-income plan." Nixon sent this proposal to Congress. If a convergence atmosphere had been in force, Capitol Hill's Democrats and Republicans might have come together to discover that such a plan deserved passage. It never happened. Divergence reigned.

Once liberals begin to admit to some of their own shortcomings, they might look at their conservative counterparts and begin to learn that not only do conservatives have their own faults—this liberals already know—but they also have beliefs that are compatible with liberal thought.

Conservatives Divided

While in the Nixon days conservatives and liberals could not agree, this is not to say that conservatives themselves have been seeing eye to eye, then or now.

When Ronald Reagan—the Right's all-time political hero—came along, he disappointed his more right-wing backers with arms control deals with the Soviet Union, raising taxes after lowering them, and, despite his antigovernment rhetoric, not reducing Big

Government or its expenditures. He greatly increased the military budget and further tanked the regulatory agencies, but he never submitted a balanced budget proposal to Congress in his eight deficit-spiraling years in office. The hardcore Right accused Reagan of deserting the cause of anticommunism after his meeting with Mikhail Gorbachev, the architect of Russia's perestroika. Reagan in his diaries implied that movement conservatives had misread him from the start. "I remind them," he wrote, "I voted for FDR 4 times. I'm trying to undo the 'Great Society,' not the New Deal."[4]

Today's radical Republicans in Congress are trying to undo the New Deal. As Garry Wills has written, "Conservatism looks to the cohesion and continuity of society—what makes people band together and remain together with some satisfaction." Wills obviously is losing some self-styled conservative leaders with that definition and many more self-described libertarians, whom Wills imperiously called people who live "in a dream world of hypothetical atoms interacting with each other dynamically. No society can ever be formed on the basis of individualism, togetherness deriving from apartness."[5]

If Garry Wills believes that libertarians do not value "continuity and stability," Russell Kirk went even further by considering libertarianism a threat to the republic. He said, writes Carl Bogus, "Libertarians believe that society revolves around 'self-interest, closely joined to the nexus of cash payment,' but that conservatives see society as 'a community of souls, joining the dead, the living, and those yet unborn' and cohering 'through what Aristotle called friendship and Christians call love of neighbor.'"[6] Further, "to talk of forming a league or coalition," wrote Kirk, "between these two is like advocating a union of ice and fire."[7] It was not clear who was fire and who was ice.

Conservatives United Under False Colors

But the point here is that divisions between those whom liberals classify under the conservative umbrella are sharp, ongoing, and sometimes vicious, except when they are muted under the current superdome of corporatism, which twists those so labeled and so tempted in accordance with its timely imperatives, getting them to buy into its version of conservatism. That is to say that today's right-wing governors, senators, and representatives mostly derive their compass from corporatism first and foremost, however much they attempt to connect what they are doing and not doing to previous political and philosophical high holders of the conservative banners. The corresponding temptation of liberal politicians also must choose between corporatism and their liberal antecedents. Once this reality is recognized, then the cards can be placed on the table for public deliberation, unencumbered by corporatists constantly recruiting both conservatives and liberals to adhere to their "principles."

Politicians always search for high-level references and plausible public explanations for their unsavory, often unlawful, or cruel decisions. House Speaker John Boehner and Senate Minority Leader Mitch McConnell have delivered enough short paragraphs with such references and explanations to a ditto-heading congressional press corps in recent years to demonstrate the importance of separating them from their facades and extracting their messages from their plausible packaging. Both start explaining their recent decisions with phrases such as "The American people are fed up with too much taxation, spending, and regulation." If an intrepid reporter persists and asks a follow-up question as to why these political leaders are really taking this position, the staccato reply is "jobs, jobs, jobs" (but not wages) or "small business" (but not Big Business). No mention of "profits, profits, profits," or "corporate power" or "executive bonuses" or "campaign contributions" or "the decision favors my leisure-time-supporting friends." If all else fails to persuade, the stopper is trotted out: "conservative values on which this country was built." Take away that doctrinal foundation, and the expedient house of cards begins to collapse and reveal: "These emperors have no clothes."

Conservatives with Principles

Yet, as this book has repeatedly underlined, there are conservatives who take their heritage seriously and fight shy of corporate influences. Among such authentic conservatives can be placed the writers John R. E. Bliese, author of *The Greening of Conservative America* (2002), and Gordon Durnil, who penned *The Making of a Conservative Environmentalist* (1995).[8] Both have as their aims the restoration and conservation for posterity of the planet—its air, water, and soil—using means that accord with conservative policies and mechanisms. They do not start out with the corporatist premise: we must do what is best for preserving the priorities of corporate hegemony, sales, profits, and bonuses.

More recently, Roger Scruton, the British philosopher and conservative intellectual, wrote a book elevatedly titled *How to Think Seriously About the Planet,* in which he asserted that "conservatism and environmentalism are natural bedfellows." He champions "English tort law" as an effective mechanism for forcing businesses to internalize the toxic effects of some of their activities. But he devalues international treaties, like the Kyoto accords, as well as centralized bureaucratic dictates that replace local solutions and civic efforts. He sees that markets fail to make companies pay for the cost of environmental pollution and damage they cause. Scruton believes in the gestational effects of two important sentiments—love of home (what the Greeks called *oikophilia*) and love of beauty, whether of "the wilderness or roads without litter." Reverberating with the thought of Edmund Burke, author Scruton asserts that "no large-scale project will succeed if it is not rooted in our small-scale practical reasoning. . . . For it is we in the end who have to act, who have to accept and co-operate with the decisions made in our name, and who have to make whatever sacrifices will be required for the sake of future generations."[9]

Then Scruton goes programmatically deeper into treacherous territory, breaking decisively with those relentless growth advocates who otherwise share his philosophical label, saying, "What is needed is not more growth but less." Furthermore, ponder his windup, in which he chides conservatives who see "consumerism and technophilia as integral to the 'market solutions' that must be protected from the socialist state. In fact, it is precisely in the fight against consumerism that left and right should be united, establishing an alliance on behalf of the environment that would also heal the rift in our civilization."[10]

Patrick Buchanan, a Populist Conservative

While unbiased liberals will see the common ground with these authors, it should be noted that there are also opportunities for convergence with that school of conservative thought deemed "populist conservatives." The group has been most articulately championed and transmitted over the mass media by Patrick J. Buchanan and finds abundant exposition in his challenging book *Where the Right Went Wrong: How Neoconservatives Subverted the Reagan Revolution and Hijacked the Bush Presidency*. Full of pertinent quotations and historical references, the book expounds Buchanan's belief that the cause of true conservatism—that of Robert Taft, Barry Goldwater, and Ronald Reagan—is being betrayed by the twin forces of neoconservatives and global corporations through three critical subversions.

First, US corporate globalization has shattered the domestic economy and the lives of its workers by exporting industries abroad under the auspices of NAFTA and the WTO treaties. "The Republican Party," declares Buchanan, "which had presided over America's rise to manufacturing preeminence, has acquiesced in the deindustrialization of the nation to gratify transnational corporations whose oligarchs are the party financiers. U.S. corporations are shutting factories here, opening them in China, [and] 'outsourcing' back-office work to India."[11]

As a win-win proposition for the United States, "free trade is a bright, shining lie," according to Buchanan.[12] Ever larger trade deficits, now reaching three-quarters of a trillion dollars a year, mean the United States is exporting jobs, consuming more than it is producing, and becoming far and away the world's largest debtor. When Federal Reserve chair Alan Greenspan was asked whether he thought the US trade deficits were harmful, his reply was: only if they persist. Well, how about our trade deficits in goods with other nations for the last thirty-seven years in a row?

In 1996, I sent letters to the largest hundred US-chartered corporations asking if they would institute a policy whereby at their annual shareholders meeting, the CEO and president would rise and in the name of the corporation—be it GM, Pfizer, DuPont, or any other—not in the name of the board of directors, pledge "allegiance to the flag . . . with liberty and justice for all." Only one company, Federated Department Stores, thought it was unequivocally a good idea. Others said they would take it under consideration or rejected the proposal or did not respond. When I released all the responses from the companies (over sixty of them) to the media, only one columnist, out of dozens of liberal, progressive, libertarian, and conservative syndicated columnists, made any mention of this minimal test of corporate patriotism. It was Buchanan, who devoted his column to the packet of responses from the company officials, ending with the question: "If they cannot pledge loyalty to America, why should Americans be loyal to them?"[13]

A convergence that would speak out against corporate managed global trade, as written in the autocratic rules of NAFTA and the WTO, is not a predictable left-of-center position. Raised on Economics 101 and the nineteenth-century theory of comparative advantage, most economists, reporters, liberal editors, writers, authors, and politicians have become knee-jerk ditto-heads when they hear the term "free trade." From the *New York Times* corporate globalization cheerleader Thomas Friedman to trade-can-do-no-harm economists like Larry Summers and Jagdish Bhagwati, the mantra is trade über alles. It does not impress them that modern globalization is facilitating "absolute advantage"— that is, the location in one or more countries of all factors of production—labor, capital, technology, and managerial skills. The real-world problems with this comparative advantage theory led free trader, MIT professor, and Nobel Laureate Paul Samuelson to write, near the end of his career, a liberal argument for reconsidering this Ricardian trade dogma.[14]

A combination of populist conservatives, industrial unionists, and smart progressives could form the convergence alliance to start the long march toward prudent economic self-reliance and away from extreme dependency fostered by globally linked financial speculators like Goldman Sachs. A drive to replace the stripmining of our domestic economy by international agreements framed and used by global corporations to exploit workers, consumers, and the environment is long overdue, given how our country is chronically slipping.

The second subversion Buchanan ascribed to the neoconservatives is that they, in the name of Republican conservatism, have plunged this nation headlong into a global empire of control, military bases, invasions, and imperial dashing of national sovereignties. Gone is the traditional, prudent conservative concern over deficits and military adventurism. The new doctrine, he avers, was contained in George W. Bush's June 2, 2002, speech at West Point establishing the new principle of the United States' right to preemptive attack and preventive war anywhere in the world. Buchanan accurately says that "the Constitution does not empower the president to launch preventive wars." He goes on, "in dealing with nations, containment and deterrence had never failed us. We contained Stalin and Mao, though both had large arsenals of nuclear weapons."[15]

President Obama has extended the Bush doctrine by declaring his unilateral right, as secret prosecutor, judge, jury, and executioner, to destroy anybody, anywhere in the world, including American citizens, suspected to be engaged in alleged terrorist activities, all this vaguely and loosely defined as anti-US security. This allows for unbridled, secret discretion contrary to the exclusive congressional authority to declare and finance wars!

The third rupture of conservative principles, according to Buchanan, is the takeover or hijacking of the Republican Party of Taft, Goldwater, and Reagan by both the neocons and the corporatists, who, for similar and dissimilar reasons, have combined to destroy our sovereignty, our constitutional restraints, and our reasonable economic self-determination. Their national security strategy has ushered in, he states, "an era of what historian Harry Elmer Barnes called 'Perpetual War for Perpetual Peace.'" A continual state of belligerence confirms President Eisenhower's final warning to his country about the insatiable, profitable "military-industrial complex."[16]

The Possibility of Convergence Keeps Raising Its Head

The possibility for convergence of populist conservatives like Buchanan with liberals and progressives is strongly based on writings, such as those to which I have just referred, and on the polls that continually show, in spite of the domination of belligerent official propaganda, at least half and sometimes up to 70 percent of the American people are not buying these endless wars and hostilities for no clearly perceived objectives. Pursue attackers and bring them to justice? Yes, they say. But year after year of widening quagmires and their blowback make Americans think more about what Ron Paul called "minding our own business," and our tending to neglected domestic conditions and needs.

Retired general Anthony Zinni, a Pentagon Middle East expert and former Centcom commander, worked with neoconservatives in the Department of Defense and found that they, with the decisive collaborators at the Bush-Cheney White House, prompted the web of deception that poured half a million US soldiers into a devastated Iraq for years. He writes: "The more I saw the more I thought this *was* the product of the neocons, who didn't understand the region and were going to create havoc there. These were dilettantes from Washington think tanks who never had an idea that worked on the ground."[17]

His strictures do not apply to the Cato Institute libertarian think tank, however, which consistently opposed the war on Iraq in detailed policy papers before and during the invasion and occupation.

But to Move to Convergence, It Is Necessary to Separate Corporatists from the Principled

In sum, it is clear that when it comes to the world of these professional conservatives, little is clear. It is all jumbled up with factions, dissenters, and claimants to the true mantle of conservatism, each providing energetic rationales for their positions and proclaiming their fealty to their intellectual forebears. The unspoken divergence of some of these factions often hinges on how lucrative their commercially connected activities are, ones that include such considerations as consulting and lecture fees, future career moves, and links to overlapping boards of directors. If it is remarkable—and it is—how hard-line and inflexible are today's Republican leaders and their flock in Congress, compared with the more independent-minded Smiths, Hayeks, von Mises, Tafts, Kirks, even Jack Kemps and Goldwaters, it is due in part to the fragility of the conservatism they tout, which cannot withstand temptations offered by corporate contributions and the rewards awaiting after retirements or electoral defeats. Infamous corporate lobbyist Jack Abramoff said, "When a public servant has a debt to someone seeking a favor from the government, the foundation of our government is at risk."[18]

Today, the traditional cloak of conservatism has been transformed into a fig leaf for the likes of Boehner, Cantor, and McConnell. Boehner is so corporate-indentured that we crafted a poster of him with his suit emblazoned with many corporate logos of those sponsoring him, from Sallie Mae to ExxonMobil. They covered every available space on his garment (see http://suitsforsale.org). He delivered for them to the utmost of his power. After all, corporatism requires that both conservatives and liberals compromise their dedicated principles in return for that proverbial "mess of pottage."

To work at all, convergence must derive from general principles, which interpret realities in ways that produce a broad agreement, with similar or different reasons being given different weights by either side. Such convergences will be welcomed by the public. On the other hand, no alliance driven by Mammon or self-enrichment can earn the allegiance of the public it is being constructed to serve. To be influential on policymakers at the top and with the citizenry behind it at the bedrock of our society, convergence must be the joining of two historic streams of cultural or societal values to change harmful realities on the ground—with no corrosive, conflicting hidden agendas.

Corporate lobbies have an effective way of putting their agendas first. They know how distracting this can be to the forces of good. Who has the time or inclination for convergence if your forces on the right are arrayed against the forces on the left over such hot-button, time-sensitive matters as major government contracts; subsidies; construction permits; licenses; tax breaks; unions; deregulation drives; earmarks; judgeships; reproductive rights; loan guarantees; revisions of Medicare, Medicaid, and Social Security; war policies; and the national security state? Both sides have chosen to spend their energies and appeal to their funders on such matters, not to mention that they inevitably are deeply engaged in primaries, elections, and struggles over campaign contributions.

Companies and their ever-hyping trade associations, backed by large law firms and public relations organizations, are forever enlisting and rewarding their allies in these struggles at the national, state, and local levels of government. Given these intense ongoing battles with no end, and their aggregation into Left-Right antagonisms, convergence efforts take a back seat. Although the contentious issues will differ, the same low priority is accorded to local convergent proposals.

And what happens to the hapless citizens who are committed to one side or another and look for cues from their accepted leaders? Are they to be relegated to await their leaders, or can they get something started on their own and up the pressure? Obviously, it does happen when there are common material interests of the improving Main Street or the neighborhood variety. For purposes of this volume, I am referring to local convergence all the way up to those national projects, such as the law putting air bags in cars (described in chapter 3).

10

Dear Billionaire

To effectuate the top-down and bottom-up dynamic of effective convergence that moves from thought to action, from being to doing, will take more than polemics. It will take a climbing of the steps, moving ever closer to culmination. This means labor-intensive work, media of different kinds, full-time organizers, and most importantly new institutions just devoted to convergences. All this in turn requires direct resources of a magnitude and consistency that will allow convergers to weather not just the inevitable problems of start-ups but also the storm of the certain opposition.

Perhaps the best way to present the case for resources is to write a hypothetical letter to a relatively enlightened, nonreclusive mega-billionaire in an era in which such super-rich are increasing their numbers and their social consciousness. Warren Buffett and Bill Gates Jr. are first among the 114 billionaires and mega-billionaires who signed a pledge to give away at least half their wealth to "good causes." When you look at their website (http://givingpledge.org), you'll see that just on this list are possibilities that would take us beyond tilting at windmills. So here we go.

Dear Super-Rich Friend:

We are sending you this book on the subject of the likelihood
and benefits of a Left-Right convergence that would act to bring
to existence important but neglected redirections or reforms in
our country. You will note that when unlikely forces, historically
and continually at odds over other political, economic, and
social issues, decide to band together, their combined power can
be decisive in unjamming long-prevailing logjams that block
needed change and could be instituted locally, nationally, and
internationally. There is something purifying and serious about
ideological opposites applying their guiding principles to come
together and get something done for a change.

Working together, they give cover to their legislative allies,
who need that cover to persuasively explain to their constituents
back home why they have allied themselves with and given
credibility to their traditional, often demonized adversaries.

The convergers also bring together different arguments and
invoke different traditions to make their cases much stronger. As
unlikely partners willing to take political capital away from their
usual contentious pursuits, they are likely to secure more media
for their combined causes. This was the case with the Left-Right
convergence to end the Breeder Reactor boondoggle described in
the opening chapter and the repeal of "cartel regulation" of the
transportation industry by Democrats and Republicans in the 1970s.

Indirectly, but importantly, they are broadening the public
discourse so as to address reality rather than allow their ideology
to deny what is actually going on. As Aldous Huxley said: "Facts
do not cease to exist because they are ignored." Those words are
truer today than when he said them back in the 1930s, given
the continuing, intensifying rigidity of positions over grave
matters of state, democracy, and economy, often taken to favor
partisan party domination or to boost other kinds of self-serving
hierarchical supremacies.

In the previous pages I have tried to make a case that convergences can become realities, and that there is much to converge over, which will break our paralysis as a country. We have, as a society, many solutions—procedural, substantive, and technical—that are not being applied to problems that we have and do not deserve. I refer you to Chapter 4 for a short menu.

In late 2012, I had two meetings with certified conservatives, one with investigative author and advocate Brink Lindsey of the Cato Institute and one with Stephen Erickson, president of the nonprofit Clean Government Alliance. Mr. Erickson, who exudes energy, sent me a seventeen-page white paper designed to put forth priority convergences and noted the strategic, organizational, and marketing steps to get the missions moving. We discussed three choices to get underway: (1) a clean elections system, requiring a constitutional amendment, given contrary Supreme Court decisions equaling money with freedom of speech; (2) an end to gerrymandering that cynically entrenches one-party district domination; and (3) reasonable congressional term limits to allow fresh energies reflecting public sentiments.

By contrast, my meeting with Brink Lindsey of the Cato Institute, a large center of disparate conservatives, included Jeff Faux, a progressive economist who started and for years ran the Economic Policy Institute, and Andy Shallal, a successful entrepreneurial restaurateur in Washington, DC, operating five innovative eateries, with public events and bookstores, called Busboys and Poets. Talking to Mr. Lindsey, I learned that he was not that interested in Mr. Erickson's choices. He cited as his priorities revising the PATRIOT Act to protect civil liberties; confronting the bloated military budget and the empire it funds, starting with a mandatory annual audit of the Pentagon budget that the Congress never gets around to assuring; and ending corporate welfare that conservatives call "crony capitalism." All of us around the table had no objection to these candidates for convergence.

Earlier I observed that convergence needs its own organizations, because it will remain third fiddle if it relies on people in the opposing organizations to take time, connections, and reputation away from their programmatic identities to work with longtime adversaries—even though it is exactly through them joining these unlikely combinations that worthy but long-inert proposals can be raised to dynamic visibility. What is required, in my experience of working and observing convergent efforts, are convergence-only organizations in which there are no other overriding priorities and images interfering with the determined mission at hand. Even single-issue groups that substantively should and could converge are reluctant to do so because of the suspicions about such convergence raised by their constituents and contributors, small and large.

So here is where my request to you becomes more specific. Substantial financial resources are necessary to make convergence a national movement that means what it says and that is capable of covering increasing numbers of subjects and withstanding the anticipated opposition.

Step 1 would be to commission writings and videos on past and current convergences. These would show the potential for greatly increasing the number and the gravity of the issues over which groups could converge so as to produce a historic realignment of civic and political forces, thereby allowing them to escape from their present toxic or static conditions.

Step 2 is to support national and local convocations to deliberate and tentatively agree on selected concrete convergent actions, with suitable proclamations for public discourse.

Step 3 is to use careful preparation to establish organizations dedicated to achieving specific missions at all levels of our political economy.

You may be asking, one can hope, about the calendar for any such involvement on your part. That is significantly a

function of how many resources are available, together with
how they can be employed with prudent absorptive capacity and
strategy by the doers. The more there are, the more synergy is
produced. Historically overdue change needs to come quickly
once initiated, otherwise the forces of the *status quo* will have
time to game the strategies of delay and obfuscation. Universal
health insurance was seriously proposed by President Harry
Truman to Congress, and we're still waiting through the sixty-
seventh year and counting for this to come to pass. By contrast,
auto safety legislation was heard, deliberated, and enacted with
overwhelming convergence by Congress within nine months
after the publication of *Unsafe at Any Speed*. It was put into law
at a signing ceremony at the White House in September 1966 by
President Lyndon Johnson.

As you know from your own business experience, enlightened
companies often do not take positions on matters they believe are
good for the country because of the fear of alienating a portion of
their employees, shareholders, supply chain partners, or consumers.
Convergence can give some cover to these companies as it does for
lawmakers. Some corporate statesmanship or corporate patriotism
can come alive with such stimuli. There is much consensus in this
country that will be seen at the grassroots, once the fog of abstract
or manipulated polarization is cleared away.

My colleagues and I seek a meeting with you to go over
what is obviously a number of questions you will have in order
to reach a level of rigor, which you rightfully are going to
demand. There is an expectation that needs to be conveyed at
the outset, however. The requested budget from you, together
with any of your colleagues you may enlist, will be in the tens
of millions of dollars, subject to strict controls, reporting, and
stages of expenditure. The frame of mind we must enter into
together, should you be interested enough to continue this
exchange and desire to communicate the value of the endeavor

to your associates, is in a way comparable to that of industrialists striving to convince investors to commit enough capital for, say, a large steel mill. The factory could not be built without a critical mass of investment money. The same holds true with this promising endeavor of multiple convergences and their expected momentums for a better country and world.

However, unlike a factory investment in which all could be lost, the convergence initiative has so many locales and redirections available that the real question would be: How much will it succeed? For the civic investment contemplated here is both to build local alliances that then attach to state and national drives for change and to start nationally and work through to the local for a mobilized convergence. Where to start would depend on the nature of the project. In this manner, we will be able to use a variety of dynamics and to recognize that some starts are better at one end of the continuum or the other. For example, the physical fitness project described in Chapter 5 is a natural for local originations and local competitions. The renovation and upgrade of public works in our deferred-maintenance country, especially given where much of the funds must come from, invite a nationwide inspiration with local convergences of business, labor, civic, charitable, and municipal groups as well as individuals.

Abraham Lincoln once memorably said, "A house divided against itself cannot stand." Today it can be said, "A house divided against itself cannot thrive." Just why people oppose each other or do not work together because of contending abstractions or "isms" in our country has been studied too abstractly as well. (An exception is Professor Howard Gardner's *Changing Minds*.) It is when means and ends are taken down to concrete levels of scrutiny and examination that fusion comes over the horizon, that the agendas of the influential few—partisan, commercial, turf-holding, fearful, and unknowing—come to the forefront for honest appraisals by themselves and the daunted many. Often convergence is not compromise as much as it is putting together two nearly identical positions that have been separated by other conflicts.

To imagine is to envision real possibilities that can perpetuate themselves in their own right. We look forward to your reactions.

Best Wishes,
Ralph Nader and the Convergers
Visit www.nader.org for more information.

Epilogue

This work has emphasized the convergence of seemingly disparate ideologies on concrete projects and programs for change.
John Kenneth Galbraith—the eminent economist for progressive reforms—once wrote that the most vested of all interests are
vested interests in ideas.[1] He was probably thinking of those historic opponents espousing capitalism, socialism, communism, or
the regulatory state versus the unfettered free market economy
or the monetarists versus the fiscalists. Actually, the defenders of
these positions tend to employ more rigid dogmas than do those
with the political labels of conservative, liberal, libertarian, or progressive. People who label themselves with the latter designations
are far more likely to converge than the true believers in "isms."

Recognized leaders of these liberal and conservative political
philosophies, whether they are thinker-scholars, elected representatives, popularizing polemicists, or popular entertainers who
speak out, as Ronald Reagan did in his preelective career, have
large numbers of like-minded followers in elections, legislatures,
or city councils. People follow the cues of these leaders, or they
follow the "influentials" in their neighborhood or community who
relay these preferences, complete with affirmative phrasings and

swipes at the opposition. At infrequent times, as suggested, the dynamic can start with the people and bubble up. AARP's leaders in Washington, who supported certain disputed legislation, found this out from their members a few years ago to their astonishment.

But at least in today's type of top-down political economy and media, when people see the leaders with whom they share strong convictions shift gears, they are far more likely to support the new directions than they would be if they simply heard a debate in which strong arguments are made on either side. This, writes law professor Cass Sunstein, is because people hearing a debate only take in information in a fashion to further bolster their long-held viewpoint. According to Sunstein, people are more likely to accept challenging information if it "comes from a trusted source they cannot dismiss," because they have regularly agreed with that leader or opinion maker. Sunstein gives as examples if "civil rights leaders oppose affirmative action, or if well-known climate change skeptics say that they were wrong, people are more likely to change their views."[2] President Lyndon Johnson understood this point intimately. When CBS network anchor Walter Cronkite—a highly credible and popular news broadcaster—returned from Vietnam and surprisingly reported to a mass audience that our war there was unwinnable, Johnson told a confidant that the battle for public opinion in America on the war was over.

Sunstein concludes that *who* says something can matter a great deal more than simply putting out the information for anyone to absorb. When retired Marine general Anthony Zinni told the *Washington Post* that it was a serious mistake to invade Iraq, the *Post* reporter added "that he hasn't received a single negative response from military people about the stance he has taken." Zinni continued, "I was surprised by the number of uniformed guys, all ranks, who said, 'You're speaking for us. Keep on keeping on.'"[3] What Zinni was saying was being said by many peace advocates, progressive writers, and some Democrats in Congress. But Zinni saying it changed the minds of those who never would have accepted the same arguments from liberals, progressives, or libertarians.

Zinni, Cronkite, and others who refuse to censor themselves and go against what is expected of them are critically sensible assets in a society in which we are told again and again of our "partisan divides," our "red" and "blue" states, and how polls show us to be poles apart on so many issues.

The media, of course, can play a major role in diffusing the news of incipient convergences. However, the media's DNA is attached to conflict, controversy, and visible disruption. Thus, the Tea Party and Occupy Wall Street received coverage because they were loudly making either unusual demands or thunderous declarations. When some Tea Partiers and the Occupy Wall Streeters got together and discovered common ground on such matters as a call for no more bailouts and violations of civil liberties, there was very little coverage, certainly less than if they had a shouting match throwing soft tomatoes at each other on the corner of Wall and Broad Streets. If there is no media, there is no expansion of what has hitherto not been reported to large numbers of people.

People receive motivation to continue and build if their pleas or demands are being heard by their fellow citizens. The demonstrators protesting outside the Democratic Party's national convention of 1968 in Chicago were roaring, "The whole world is watching," as the police set upon them. Well, that was the high mark of coverage by such mass corporate media—television, radio, and press—of dissenting street demonstrations. Somewhere high up in the skyscrapers, where decisions for reporting on outside political conventions and elsewhere are made, the men around the table acted in a way that meant, "Yeah, well, that's not going to happen again."

But 1968 was a long time ago, and the media has many more faces than in the days when there were only three national TV networks reaching everybody who chose to watch. At this point, convergent initiatives have to be particularly adept in moving, for what it's worth, through the fractured social media as well as in the traditional media, which still hold the greatest influence on decision-makers. Convergers have to use crisper, sharper words to make their points. They need to peacefully picket and demonstrate in the grand American tradition, not just to get attention but to enlarge their own community solidarities and laser-beam concentrations. Importantly, they must go into the dens of the legislators and the agencies of the executive branch of government to make known personally and directly their goals, and be willing to file serious lawsuits where merited.

The operational fuel for these efforts is money. Justice needs money; it always has in American history, whether for abolition of slavery and early women's rights movements or the civil rights and environmental drives of our generation. Far less than 1 percent of the affluent in today's America can put convergence on a fast track. Convergence has to be a uniquely appealing strategy to people of exceptional wealth, especially in their later years, when they have a different perspective on their own legacy. Granted, donated money can dilute, control, and even corrupt. But received with the requisite alertness and clear understanding, money can have a greatly enhanced effect in overcoming the naysayers and skeptics about anything getting done in our gridlocked country. So call, write, and meet them one on one or at group dinners. Prepare to reach only a few of them. That will be more than enough to get the train on the tracks for a sustained journey.

A sense of division of labor among convergers is enhancing. Reaching out to find the wealthy supporters needs traits associated with extroverts: sociability and gregariousness coupled with calmness and deliberation. For other functions, such as persuading media or legislators, or preparing arguments and briefs, different personalities come into play. That convergers often come with substantial experience in public advocacy does not obviate these obvious points too often ignored. Experience, it should be noted, can be antithetical to innovative, bold thinking that breaks new ground and invites new talents to emerge from settled personalities. Convergence is not for the timid. Convergence is for pioneers breaking out of cultural ruts to move to the higher planes of human agreements and achievements.

Acknowledgments

My thanks to the individuals who consented to the interviews cited throughout the book. Thank you to Jim Fiest for his thoughtful suggestions. I am grateful to John Richard and his capable associates Monica Giannone and Katherine Raymond, who went through the numerous processes set forth by the diligent editors at Nation Books, in particular Carl Bromley, before *Unstoppable* could pop out of the printing presses toward a broad-based readership.

Special thanks to the Intercollegiate Studies Institute (ISI) for keeping *Who Owns America? A New Declaration of Independence*, co-edited by Allen Tate and Herbert Agar, and so many other works by thoughtful conservatives in print. For a list of ISI publications visit http://isibooks.org/.

Notes

Introduction

1. Out of the 6,312 votes, 3,258 were cast by Republicans, 3,054 by Democrats. *Federal Elections 92: Election Results for the U.S. President, the U.S. Senate and the U.S. House of Representatives* (Washington, DC: Federal Election Commission, 1993), http://www.fec.gov/pubrec/fe1992/federal elections92.pdf.

2. Aaron Bernstein, Michael Arndt, Wendy Zellner, and Peter Coy, "Too Much Corporate Power?" *Bloomberg Businessweek*, September 11, 2000.

Chapter 1

1. Michael Ganley, "Both Sides Seeking Final Votes on Clinch River," *Environmental and Energy Study Conference Update*, September 27, 1983, 8, http://digitalcollections.library.cmu.edu/awweb/awarchive?type =file&item=430733.

2. Paul Tsongas, "Deep-Sixing Clinch River," *Christian Science Monitor*, March 18, 1983, http://www.csmonitor.com/1983/0318/031830.html/(pag)/e2.

3. Michael Ganley, "Both Sides Seeking Final Votes on Clinch River," Environmental and Energy Study Conference Update, September 27, 1983, 8, http://digitalcollections.library.cmu.edu/awweb/awarchive?type= file&item=430733; Congress Watch and Rural America are accounted for in "On Behalf of the Taxpayers Coalition Against Clinch River," letter to Committee on Science and Technology, "Fiscal Year 1984 Department of

Energy Authorization: Nuclear Fission R&D and Waste Management," US House of Representatives, 1984.

4. The sources for the $8.8 billion figure are Judith Miller, "Report Doubles Estimate of Breeder Reactor's Cost," *New York Times*, September 24, 1982, and *Interim Report on GAO's Review of the Total Cost Estimate for the Clinch River Breeder Reactor Project*, General Accounting Office, EMD-82-131, September 23, 1982; the source for the $5.3 billion to $9 billion range is "Energy and Environment," *Los Angeles Times*, September 16, 1982, SD2.

5. "Clinch River Breeder Reactor Project Dies in Congress," *Wall Street Journal*, October 27, 1983.

6. Henry Scammell, *Giantkillers: The Team and the Law That Help Whistle-Blowers Recover America's Stolen Billions* (New York: Atlantic Monthly Press, 2004), 278.

7. Fraud Statistics – Overview, October 1, 1987–September 30, 2011," Civil Division, US Department of Justice, http://www.taf.org/DoJ-fraud-stats -FY2011.pdf.

8. Interview with Bruce Fein on October 31, 2013, verifying facts.

9. Franklin D. Roosevelt, "Message to Congress on Curbing Monopolies," April 29, 1938, *The American Presidency Project*, http://www.presidency .ucsb.edu/ws/?pid=15637.

10. Peter Schweizer interview on *The Sean Hannity Show*, Fox News, April 4, 2013, http://www.foxnews.com/on-air/hannity/2013/04/08/boomtown -2-business-food-stamps.

11. George F. Will, "Rending Steel and Siren Cry Accompany Today's Song," *The Sun*, A19, April 14, 1977.

12. "Nader Says Gaming Targets Children," *Las Vegas Review-Journal*, June 13, 1998; "Making Parents Irrelevant," *Nader Page*, October 27, 1999, http://nader.org/1999/10/27/making-parents-irrelevant.

13. Republican Party of Texas Platform, 2002, 16, http://www.yuricareport .com/Dominionism/RPTPlatform2002.pdf.

14. Aldous Huxley, "A Note on Dogma," in *Proper Studies* (London: Chatto & Windus, 1927).

15. Mike Duke's pay was $23.15 million in 2012. Scott DeCarlo, "Gravity-Defying CEO Pay," *Forbes*, April 4, 2012, http://www.forbes.com/lists/2012/12 /ceo-compensation-12_land.html.

16. Lori Wallach and Michelle Sforza, *Whose Trade Organization? Corporate Globalization and the Erosion of Democracy*, Public Citizen's Global Trade Watch, October 1999, http://www.citizen.org/publications/publication redirect.cfm?ID=7081.

Chapter 2

1. Robert A. G. Monks, *The Emperor's Nightingale: Restoring the Integrity of the Corporation* (Oxford: Capstone, 1998), 13, http://www.ragm.com/libraryFiles/57.pdf.

2. Adam Smith, *The Wealth of Nations* (New York: Bantam, 2003), 110–111.

3. Ibid., 257.

4. Bruce Frohnen, Jeremy Beer, and Jeffrey O. Nelson, eds., *American Conservatism: An Encyclopedia* (Wilmington, DE: ISI Books, 2006); Murray N. Rothbard, "Ludwig von Mises (1881-1973)," The Ludwig von Mises Institute, July 27, 2005, http://mises.org/daily/1876.

5. Murray N. Rothbard, "Biography of Ludwig von Mises (1881–1973)," The Ludwig von Mises Institute, http://mises.org/page/1468/Biography-of-Ludwig-von-Mises-18811973.

6. Rothbard, "Ludwig von Mises."

7. Shawn Ritenour, "Biography of Wilhelm Röpke (1899–1966)," The Ludwig von Mises Institute, http://mises.org/page/1461/Biography-of-Wilhelm-Ropke-18991966-Humane-Economist.

8. Wilhelm Röpke, *A Humane Economy: The Social Framework of the Free Market* (Chicago: Regnery, 1960), 137, 141, http://library.mises.org/books/Wilhelm%20R246pke/A%20Humane%20Economy.pdf.

9. George Carlin once said, "The invisible hand of Adam Smith seems to offer an extended middle finger to an awful lot of people." Gavin Kennedy, "Saturday Snippets," *Adam Smith's Lost Legacy* (blog), January 3, 2009, http://adamsmithslostlegacy.blogspot.com/2009/01/saturday-snippets.html.

10. Friedrich Hayek, *The Road to Serfdom* (New York: Routledge Classics, 2005), 125.

11. Frank S. Meyer, *In Defense of Freedom: A Conservative Credo*, (Chicago: Regnery, 1962), 9.

12. Russell Kirk, *The Conservative Mind: From Burke to Eliot*, 7th rev. ed. (Washington, DC: Regnery, 1986), 490.

13. Peter Viereck, *Conservatism Revisited: The Revolt Against Ideology, 1815–1949* (New Brunswick, NJ: Transaction, 2005), 82.

14. Ibid., 142.

15. David Brooks, "Going Home Again," *New York Times*, December 29, 2011, http://www.nytimes.com/2011/12/30/opinion/going-home-again.html; Michael Gerson, "Why Reform Conservatism Deserves a Chance," *Washington Post*, April 30, 2012, http://articles.washingtonpost.com/2012-04-30/opinions/35450887_1_tea-party-entitlement-reform-premium-support-system.

16. Frank I. Luntz, "Five Myths About Conservative Voters," *Washington Post*, April 27, 2012. http://www.washingtonpost.com/opinions/five-myths -about-conservative-voters/2012/04/27/glQAFxr0IT_story.html.

17. Richard M. Scaife, "An Open Letter to Fellow Conservatives: Why Conservatives Should Oppose Efforts to Defund Planned Parenthood," n.d., http://www.politico.com/static/PPM153_aaa_040311.html; Marjorie Dannenfelser, "Scaife's Planned Parenthood Arguments Fall on Deaf Ears," http://www.redstate.com/mdannenfelser/2011/04/05/scaifes-planned -parenthood-arguments-fall-on-deaf-ears.

18. Alan Simpson, "Why the GOP Should Support Publicly Funded Campaigns," *Washington Post*, May 05, 2011, http://articles.washingtonpost .com/2011-05-05/opinions/35233097_1_campaign-finance-public-funds -campaign-money; Ryan Grim, "Alan Simpson Attacks AARP, Says Social Security Is 'Not a Retirement Program,'" *Huffington Post*, May 9, 2006, http://www.huffingtonpost.com/2011/05/06/alan-simpson-aarp-social -security-retirement-program_n_858738.html.

19. Fareed Zakaria, "Why Defense Spending Should Be Cut," *Washington Post*, August 3, 2011, http://articles.washingtonpost.com/2011-08-03 /opinions/35270749_1_defense-budget-defense-cuts-defense-expenditures.

20. Ronald McKinnon, "The Conservative Case for a Wealth Tax," *Wall Street Journal*, January 9, 2012, http://online.wsj.com/news/articles/SB100014 24052970203462304577139232881346686.

21. Jeffrey Rosen, "Review of 'Against Interpretation: Cosmic Constitutional Theory,' by J. Harvie Wilkinson III," *New York Times*, March 18, 2012, http://www.nytimes.com/2012/03/18/books/review/cosmic-constitutional -theory-by-j-harvie-wilkinson-iii.html.

22. David Brooks, "The Big Society," *New York Times*, May 19, 2011, http://www.nytimes.com/2011/05/20/opinion/20brooks.html.

23. David Brooks, "The Road Not Taken," *New York Times*, July 18, 2011, http://www.nytimes.com/2011/07/19/opinion/19brooks.html.

24. Melanie Mason and Matea Gold, "Bachmann's Had Her Share of Government Aid," *Los Angeles Times*, June 26, 2011, http://articles.latimes .com/2011/jun/26/nation/la-na-bachmann-20110626.

25. David Stockman, *The Great Deformation: The Corruption of Capitalism in America* (New York: PublicAffairs, 2013); Stephen Moore, "Bow to Our Malefactors," *Wall Street Journal*, April 17, 2013, http://online.wsj.com /news/articles/SB10001424127887324695104578415263903796402.

26. George Will, "John McCain's Never-Ending War," *Washington Post*, June 22, 2011, http://articles.washingtonpost.com/2011-06-22/opinions /35236055_1_libya-moammar-gaddafi-isolationists; George Will, "Obama's Lawless War," *Washington Post*, June 19, 2011, editorial, p. A21.

27. Patrick Buchanan, *Where the Right Went Wrong: How Neoconservatives Subverted the Reagan Revolution and Hijacked the Bush Presidency* (New York: Thomas Dunne / St. Martin's, 2004).

28. David A. Fahrenthold, "'Peace' May Never Get a Chance in House," *Washington Post*, May 20, 2012, A06.

29. Peter Viereck, *Shame and Glory of the Intellectuals: Babbitt Jr. Vs. the Rediscovery of Values* (New Brunswick, NJ: Transaction, 1965), 18.

30. Howard Gardner, *Changing Minds: The Art and Science of Changing Our Own and Other People's Minds* (Cambridge, MA: Harvard Business Press), 2004.

Chapter 3

1. H. Con. Res. 107, 112th Congress (2011-2012), http://thomas.loc.gov /cgi-bin/query/z?c112:H.CON.RES.107:.

2. See US Senate, Official Declarations of War by Congress, http:// www.senate.gov/pagelayout/history/h_multi_sections_and_teasers/War DeclarationsbyCongress.htm.

3. Gore Vidal, *Reflections Upon a Sinking Ship* (Boston: Little, Brown, 1969), 136.

4. Lee Ferran, "The $77 Billion Fighter Jets That Have Never Gone to War," ABC News, April 8, 2011, http://abcnews.go.com/Blotter/77-billion -raptor-22-fighter-jets-war/story?id=13322450; Graham Smith, "The Osprey: Good Reviews, But a Costly Program," National Public Radio, October 24, 2011, http://www.npr.org/2011/10/24/141589693/the-osprey-good -reviews-but-a-costly-program; Lee Ferran, "Multi-Billion Dollar F-35 Fleet Grounded," ABC News, Feb 22, 2013, http://abcnews.go.com/blogs /headlines/2013/02/multi-billion-dollar-f-35-fleet-grounded.

5. "'Blow the Whistle' Project: On the Media & GAP Team Up to Identify the 'Secret Hold' Senator," Government Accountability Project, n.d., http://www.whistleblower.org/action-center/secret-hold-campaign.

6. Kevin Zeese, "After Seven Years of War in Iraq, 8 Years in Afghanistan, Opposition to War Crosses the U.S. Political Spectrum," thepeoples voice.org, March 17, 2010, http://www.thepeoplesvoice.org/TPV3/Voices .php/2010/03/17/after-seven-years-of-war-in-iraq-8-years.

7. *ComeHomeAmerica.us: Historic and Current Opposition to U.S. Wars and How a Coalition of Citizens from the Political Right and Left Can End American Empire*, ed. George D. O'Neill Jr., Paul Buhle, Bill Kauffman, and Kevin Zeese (Lake Wales, FL: Titan, 2010).

8. "ABA Policy and Report on Domestic Surveillance in the Fight Against Terrorism," American Bar Association, February 13, 2006, http://apps

.americanbar.org/op/greco/memos/aba_house302-0206.pdf; "ABA Policy and Report on Presidential Signing Statements and the Separation of Powers Doctrine," American Bar Association, August 7–8, 2006, http://www .americanbar.org/content/dam/aba/migrated/leadership/2006/annual/daily journal/20060823144113.authcheckdam.pdf.

9. George Corsetti, "Poletown Revisited," *Counterpunch*, September 18–20, 2004, http://www.counterpunch.org/2004/09/18/poletown-revisited; Ralph Nader and Alan Hirsch, "Making Eminent Domain Humane," *Villanova Law Review* 49, no. 1 (2004): 207.

Chapter 5

1. "Overview: FY2014 Defense Budget," Office of the Under Secretary of Defense, April 2012, 1-1, http://comptroller.defense.gov/defbudget/fy2014 /FY2014_Budget_Request_Overview_Book.pdf.

2. "Audit: U.S. Lost Track of $9 Billion in Iraq Funds," CNN, January 31, 2005, http://edition.cnn.com/2005/WORLD/meast/01/30/iraq.audit.

3. "Defense Inventory: Opportunities Exist to Save Billions by Reducing Air Force's Unneeded Spare Parts Inventory," GAO-07-232, Government Accountability Office, April 27, 2007, http://www.gao.gov/products /GAO-07-232.

4. Howard Dean, *Let's Drive Over the Fiscal Cliff* (video), Big Think, August 14, 2012, http://bigthink.com/videos/howard-dean-lets-drive-over -the-fiscal-cliff.

5. Robert Pollin, "Making the Federal Minimum Wage a Living Wage," University of Massachusetts, 2007, http://www.peri.umass.edu/fileadmin /pdf/other_publication_types/Pollin_May_2007_NLF_Column--Making _Federal_Min_Wage_a_Living_Wage.pdf; "Letter from 100 Economists in Support of $10.50 Minimum Wage," Time for a Raise, July 2013, http:// www.timeforaraise.org/wp-content/uploads/2013/07/Economists-Petition -for-10.50-Minimum-Wage.pdf.

6. John Boehner, "A Plan for America's Job Creators," *Greenville Daily Advocate* (NC), June 11, 2011, http://www.johnboehner.com/news/plan -americas-job-creators.

7. David Corn, "Reagan: Morning After in America: Why the Gipper's Tax-Cut Guru Is Aghast at Today's GOP," *Mother Jones*, February 4, 2011, http://www.motherjones.com/politics/2011/02/reagan-anniversary -david-stockman.

8. "Tax Revenue Is at Its Lowest Level Since 1950," Center for American Progress, June, 2011, http://www.americanprogress.org/issues/2011/06/pdf /low_tax_graphs.pdf.

9. Corn, "Reagan."

10. Phillip Inman, "EU Approves Financial Transaction Tax for 11 Eurozone Countries," *Guardian* (London), January 22, 2013, http://www.theguardian .com/business/2013/jan/22/eu-approves-financial-transaction-tax-eurozone.

11. Katrina vanden Heuvel, "Stop Coddling the Big Banks," *Nation*, February 12, 2013, http://www.thenation.com/blog/172842/stop-coddling-big-banks.

12. George Will, "Too Big to Maintain?," *Washington Post*, October 12, 2012, http://articles.washingtonpost.com/2012-10-12/opinions/35501753_1 _banks-andrew-haldane-systemically-important-financial-institutions.

13. Ryan Grim, "Dick Durbin: Banks 'Frankly Own the Place," *Huffington Post*, May 30, 2009, http://www.huffingtonpost.com/2009/04/29/dick -durbin-banks-frankly_n_193010.html.

14. Ian Wilhelm, "Start-Ups of New Charities See No Slowdown in Bad Economy," *Chronicle of Philanthropy*, April 18, 2010, http://philanthropy .com/article/Great-Recession-Generates-Many/65102/.

15. David McCullough, *John Adams* (New York: Simon & Schuster, 2001), 53.

16. Ibid.

17. *Arizona Christian School Tuition Organization v. Win*, 131 S. Ct. 1436 (2011).

18. A link to the full report is available in the press release "What Works? A Review of Auto Insurance Rate Regulation in America," Consumer Federation of America, November 12, 2013, http://www.consumerfed.org/news /720.

19. "Reelection Rates Over the Years," Opensecrets.org, http://www.open secrets.org/bigpicture/reelect.php, accessed October 25, 2013.

20. Theresa Amato, *Grand Illusion: The Myth of Voter Choice in a Two-Party Tyranny* (New York: New Press, 2009).

21. Theodore J. Lowi, "Toward a More Responsible Three-Party System: Deregulating American Democracy," in *The State of the Parties: The Changing Role of Contemporary American Parties*, ed. John C. Green and Rick Farmer, 4th ed. (Lanham, MD: Rowman & Littlefield, 2003), 376.

22. James T. Bennett, *Stifling Political Competition: How Government Has Rigged the System to Benefit Demopublicans and Exclude Third Parties* (New York: Springer, 2008), 7–8.

23. Jeff Gamet, "Apple Joins Digital Due Process Coalition," *Mac Observer*, September 23, 2011, http://www.macobserver.com/tmo/article/apple _joins_digital_due_process_coalition.

24. "House Vote 412: Rejects Limits on N.S.A. Data Collection," *New York Times*, July 24, 2013, http://politics.nytimes.com/congress/votes/113/house /1/412.

25. "Trans-Pacific Partnership: A Plan for 'Corporate Global Governance," interview with Lori Wallach on *Democracy Now!*, June 15, 2012, http://www.democraticunderground.com/101734628.

26. Jeffrey D. Clements, *Corporations Are Not People: Why They Have More Rights Than You Do and What You Can Do About It* (San Francisco: Berrett-Koehler, 2011), 23.

27. Ibid.

28. Russell Kirk, "Ten Conservative Principles," The Russell Kirk Center for Cultural Renewal, http://www.kirkcenter.org/index.php/detail/ten -conservative-principles, adapted from *The Politics of Prudence* (1993).

29. Ben Stein, "On Buyouts, There Ought to Be a Law," *New York Times*, September 3, 2006, http://www.nytimes.com/2006/09/03/business/your money/03every.html.

30. Ibid.

31. David B. Resnik, *Owning the Genome: A Moral Analysis of DNA Patenting* (Albany: SUNY Press, 2004), 2.

32. Martin Teitel and Kimberly A. Wilson, *Genetically Engineered Food: Changing the Nature of Nature*, updated and expanded 2nd ed. (Rochester, VT: Park Street, 2001).

33. David Dagan and Steven M. Teles, "The Conservative War on Prisons," *Washington Monthly* (November/December 2012).

34. Dan Merica and Evan Perez, "Eric Holder Seeks to Cut Mandatory Minimum Drug Sentences," CNN, August 12, 2013, http://www.cnn.com /2013/08/12/politics/holder-mandatory-minimums/.

35. "Prison Reform: An Unlikely Alliance of Left and Right," *Economist*, August 17, 2013, http://www.economist.com/news/united-states/21583701 -america-waking-up-cost-mass-incarceration-unlikely-alliance-left-and.

36. "Prohibition Is Finally Coming to an End," The Drug Policy Institute, December 20, 2012, http://www.drugpolicy.org/news/2012/12/full-page-new -york-times-ad-thursday-paper-80-years-after-end-prohibition-prohibition-f.

37. George F. Will, "Seeking Sense on Sentencing," *Cleveland Plain Dealer*, June 13, 2013, http://www.cleveland.com/opinion/index.ssf/2013/06/ seeking_sense_on_sentencing_ge.html.

38. Peter Viereck, "Conservatism: Attitudes, Types, & Present Status," Political Education, Conservative Analysis: Politics, Society, & the Sovereign State—Website of Dr. Almon Leroy Way Jr., n.d., http://www.proconservative .net/pecapoliticalphilosophyconservatismviereck.shtml.

39. Russell Kirk, "Common Reader for Everyday Ecologists," *Times-Picayune* (New Orleans), September 20, 1971.

40. John Gray, *Beyond the New Right: Markets, Government and the Common Environment* (New York: Routledge, 2013), 122.

41. John R. E. Bliese, *The Greening of Conservative America* (Boulder: Westview, 2001), x.

42. "The Pentagon and Climate Change," *Monthly Review*, May 1, 2004, http://monthlyreview.org/2004/05/01/the-pentagon-and-climate-change.

43. Dr. Julie L. Gerberding, "Letter: More About Health, Less About Care," *Wall Street Journal*, December 18, 2008, http://online.wsj.com/news/articles/SB122956383633516883.

44. Roger Cohen, "The Beauty of Institutions," *New York Times*, October 24, 2011, http://www.nytimes.com/2011/10/25/opinion/25iht-edcohen25.html.

Chapter 6

1. William Greider, *Who Will Tell the People: The Betrayal of American Democracy* (New York: Simon & Schuster, 1993), 281.

2. Stephen Slivinski, "The Corporate Welfare Budget: Bigger Than Ever," The Cato Institute, Cato Policy Analysis No. 415, October 10, 2001, http://www.cato.org/pubs/pas/pa-415es.html; Brian M. Riedl and John E. Frydenlund, "At the Federal Trough: Farm Subsidies for the Rich and Famous," The Heritage Foundation, November 26, 2001, http://www.heritage.org/research/reports/2001/11/at-the-federal-trough-farm-subsidies-for-the-rich-and-famous.

3. Arthur C. Brooks, "Obama Says It's Only 'Fair' to Raise Taxes on the Rich; He's Wrong," *Washington Post*, April 22, 2011, http://articles.washingtonpost.com/2011-04-22/opinions/35230666_1_tax-code-budget-rhetoric-fairness-argument.

4. Ed Crane, e-mail message to author, 2011.

5. Justice Sandra Day O'Connor, "Pro Bono Work: Good News and Bad News," Address to the 1991 American Bar Association Annual Meeting, Pro Bono Awards Luncheon, August 12, 1991. Excerpts reprinted at the Nader Page, http://nader.org/1991/09/20/justice-oconnor-speech-need-for-legal-services/.

6. Ibid.

7. Ibid.

8. Ibid.

9. Matthew Mosk, "O'Connor Calls Citizens United Ruling 'A Problem,'" ABC News, January 26, 2010, http://abcnews.go.com/Blotter/oconnor-citizens-united-ruling-problem/story?id=9668044.

Chapter 7

1. Herbert Agar and Allen Tate, editors, *Who Owns America? A New Declaration of Independence*, with a new foreword by Edward S. Shapiro (Wilmington, DE: ISI Books, 1999).

2. Edward S. Shapiro, "A Forgotten American Classic," in Agar and Tate, *Who Owns America?*, ix.

3. Ibid., xiv.

4. Ibid., xviii, xix.

5. David Cushman Coyle, "The Fallacy of Mass Production," in Agar and Tate, *Who Owns America?*, 27.

6. Lyle H. Lanier, "Big Business in the Property State," in Agar and Tate, *Who Owns America?*, 38.

7. John C. Rawe, "Agriculture and the Property State," in Agar and Tate, *Who Owns America?*, 71.

8. Ibid., 65.

9. Lyle H. Lanier, "Big Business in the Property State," in Agar and Tate, *Who Owns America?*, 30–31.

10. Ibid., 31.

11. Allen Tate, "Notes on Liberty and Property," in Agar and Tate, *Who Owns America?*, 122, 125.

12. Lanier, "Big Business," 44.

13. Ibid., 50.

14. Ibid., 47.

15. Ibid., 53, 61.

16. Herbert Agar, "But Can It Be Done?," in Agar and Tate, *Who Owns America?*, 130.

17. Ibid., 131.

18. Ibid., 132.

19. David Cho, "A Skeptical Outsider Becomes Bush's 'Wartime General,'" *Washington Post*, November 19, 2008.

20. Mary Shattuck Fisher, "The Emancipated Woman," in Agar and Tate, *Who Owns America?*, 401.

21. Ibid., 408.

22. Ibid., 410, 411.

23. T. J. Cauley, "The Illusion of State," in Agar and Tate, *Who Owns America?*, 376, 377.

24. Ibid., 367.

25. Jesse Eisinger, "As Banking Titans Reflect on Errors, Few Pay Any Price," *New York Times*, August 2, 2012, http://query.nytimes.com/2012/08/01/few-repercussions-in-the-conversion-of-a-former-wall-st-titan/.

26. William D. Cohan, "Rethinking Robert Rubin," *Bloomberg Businessweek*, September 30, 2012, http://www.businessweek.com/articles/2012-09-19/rethinking-robert-rubin.

27. Shapiro, "*Who Owns America?*," 44.

28. Franklin Roosevelt's Address Announcing the Second New Deal, October 31, 1936, FDR Library, Marist College, http://docs.fdrlibrary.marist.edu /od2ndst.html.

29. Shapiro, "*Who Owns America?*," 43.

30. Aliteracy is the state of being able to read but being uninterested in doing so. This phenomenon has been reported as a problem occurring separately from illiteracy, which is more common in the developing world, while aliteracy is primarily a problem in the developed world.

Chapter 8

1. F. A. Hayek, *The Road to Serfdom: Text and Documents—The Definitive Edition* (Chicago: University of Chicago Press, 2009), 87, Google Books edition.

2. Carl T. Bogus, *Buckley: William F. Buckley Jr. and the Rise of American Conservatism* (New York: Bloomsbury, 2011), 135–136.

3. *Changing America: Blueprints for the New Administration: The Citizens Transition Project*, edited by Mark Green (New York: Newmarket, 1992), 30.

4. Adam Davidson, "Prime Time for Paul Ryan's Guru (the One Who's Not Ayn Rand)," *New York Times*, August 21, 2012, http://www.nytimes.com /2012/08/26/magazine/prime-time-for-paul-ryans-guru-the-one-thats-not -ayn-rand.html.

5. Russell Kirk, "Review of Democracy and Leadership (Babbitt) and Great Humanists (Hough)," *Western Political Quarterly* (June 7, 1954): 296–299; reprinted on the Imaginative Conservative, http://www.theimaginative conservative.org/2011/05/kirks-review-of-democracy-and.html.

6. Henry Calvert Simons, *A Positive Program for Laissez Faire: Some Proposals for a Liberal Economic Policy* (Chicago: University of Chicago Press, 1949).

7. *Changing America*, 31.

8. James T. Patterson, *Mr. Republican: A Biography of Robert A. Taft* (Boston: Houghton Mifflin, 1972) 155.

9. Bogus, *Buckley*, 29.

10. Patterson, *Mr. Republican*, 319.

11. Ibid., 323.

12. Ibid., 331.

Chapter 9

1. Jeff Faux, e-mail message to author.

2. Robert Brent Toplin, *Radical Conservatism: The Right's Political Religion* (Lawrence: University Press of Kansas, 2006), 265.

3. Nicholas D. Kristof, "Profiting from a Child's Illiteracy," *New York Times*, December 7, 2012, http://www.nytimes.com/2012/12/09/opinion/sunday/kristof-profiting-from-a-childs-illiteracy.html.

4. Ronald Reagan, *The Reagan Diaries* (New York: HarperCollins, 2009), 65.

5. Garry Wills, *Confessions of a Conservative* (New York: Penguin Books, 1980), 210.

6. Carl T. Bogus, *Buckley: William F. Buckley Jr. and the Rise of American Conservatism* (New York: Bloomsbury, 2011), 139–140.

7. Russell Kirk, *Redeeming the Time*, ed. Jeffrey O. Nelson (Wilmington, DE: Intercollegiate Studies Institute, 1996), 271.

8. John Bliese, *The Greening of Conservative America* (Boulder: Westview, 2002); Gordon Durnil, *The Making of a Conservative Environmentalist* (Bloomington: Indiana University Press, 1995).

9. Roger Scruton, *How to Think Seriously About the Planet: The Case for an Environmental Conservatism* (New York: Oxford University Press, 2012), 9, 2.

10. Ibid., 246.

11. Patrick J. Buchanan, *Where the Right Went Wrong: How Neoconservatives Subverted the Reagan Revolution and Hijacked the Bush Presidency* (New York: Macmillan, 2007), 7.

12. Ibid., 171.

13. Patrick J. Buchanan, "Patriotism in the Boardroom," June 30, 1998, http://buchanan.org/blog/pjb-patriotism-in-the-boardroom-319.

14. Robert Kuttner, "Rethinking Free Trade," *Boston Globe*, September 29, 2004.

15. Buchanan, *Where the Right Went Wrong*, 21.

16. Ibid., 28; "The Military–Industrial Complex; The Farewell Address of President Eisenhower," 1961, http://coursesa.matrix.msu.edu/~hst306/documents/indust.html.

17. Thomas E. Ricks, "For Vietnam Vet Anthony Zinni, Another War on Shaky Territory," *Washington Post*, December 23, 2003, C1, http://www.washingtonpost.com/wp-dyn/articles/A22922-2003Dec22_3.html.

18. Jack Abramoff, "I Know the Congressional Culture of Corruption," *Atlantic*, July 24, 2012.

Epilogue

1. Stephen P. Dunn, *The Economics of John Kenneth Galbraith: Introduction, Persuasion, and Rehabilitation* (Cambridge: Cambridge University Press, 2011), 44.

2. Cass R. Sunstein, "Breaking Up the Echo," *New York Times*, September 17, 2012, http://www.nytimes.com/2012/09/18/opinion/balanced-news-reports-may-only-inflame.html.

3. Thomas E. Ricks, "For Vietnam Vet Anthony Zinni, Another War on Shaky Territory," *Washington Post*, December 23, 2003, C1, http://www.washingtonpost.com/wp-dyn/articles/A22922-2003Dec22_3.html.

Index

Credit: Beverly Orr

Ralph Nader is an author, a lecturer, an attorney, and an American political activist in areas of consumer and worker protection, humanitarianism, environmentalism, and democratic government. He is the best-selling author of many books, including *Unsafe at Any Speed*, a critique of the safety record of American automobile manufacturers. Nader is a four-time candidate for president of the United States, having run as the Green Party nominee in 1996 and 2000 and as an independent candidate in 2004 and 2008.

The Nation Institute

Founded in 2000, **Nation Books** has become a leading voice in American independent publishing. The inspiration for the imprint came from the *Nation* magazine, the oldest independent and continuously published weekly magazine of politics and culture in the United States.

The imprint's mission is to produce authoritative books that break new ground and shed light on current social and political issues. We publish established authors who are leaders in their area of expertise, and endeavor to cultivate a new generation of emerging and talented writers. With each of our books we aim to positively affect cultural and political discourse.

Nation Books is a project of The Nation Institute, a nonprofit media center dedicated to strengthening the independent press and advancing social justice and civil rights. The Nation Institute is home to a dynamic range of programs: the award-winning Investigative Fund, which supports ground-breaking investigative journalism; the widely read and syndicated website TomDispatch; the Victor S. Navasky Internship Program in conjunction with the *Nation* magazine; and Journalism Fellowships that support up to 25 high-profile reporters every year.

For more information on Nation Books, The Nation Institute, and the *Nation* magazine, please visit:

www.nationbooks.org

www.nationinstitute.org

www.thenation.com

www.facebook.com/nationbooks.ny

Twitter: @nationbooks